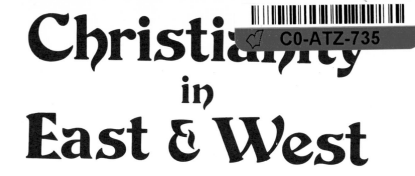

Christianity in
in
East & West

Christopher Dawson

EDITED BY JOHN J. MULLOY

Sherwood Sugden & Company
PUBLISHERS

1117 Eighth Street, La Salle, Illinois 61301

Sherwood Sugden & Company, Publishers
1117 Eighth Street
La Salle, Illinois 61301

Contents

Foreword

by John J. Mulloy

The present volume is an expanded version of *The Movement of World Revolution*, which was published in 1959, two years after the appearance of the synthesis volume of Christopher Dawson's thought, *Dynamics of World History*. What has been added to the 1959 volume are: (1) a chapter entitled "The Mediator Between East and West," which shows the relationship of Christianity to both Oriental and Occidental civilizations; (2) "Early Encounters Between East and West," an overall view of the way in which conquests made by rulers from either the East or the West have led to a cross-fertilization of cultures; (3) "The Papacy and the Modern World," Dawson's view of the Papacy as a center for the spiritual unity of mankind. This chapter is taken from an article written in 1956 concerning the achievement of Pope Pius XII and his papal predecessors, but events in the pontificates since then have made it even more pertinent.

For an understanding of Christopher Dawson's conception of East-West relationships, and the part played by religion in their development, the following themes are of major importance:

(1) The dynamic character of Western culture in comparison with other world cultures; it was this concept which was responsible for the original title of the volume, i.e., *The Movement of World Revolution.*

(2) The many-faceted relationship of Christianity to the cultural traditions of both East and West, in which the West is identified with Europe and the Americas, and the East not only with Farther Asia (India and China), but also with the world of the Middle East and North Africa.

(3) The specific character of Christianity, as seen through comparison with the Oriental world religions.

(4) The significance for Christianity of the present period in world history, as a result of the breaking down of the cultural barriers which formerly separated East and West. This has created a situation in which Christianity, Communism, secular humanism, and possibly some revised form of Oriental religion, are rivals to become the principle of unity in the cosmopolitan society of the future.

The first theme attributes the dynamic character of Western culture especially to the formative influence of the Christian Faith. Dawson points out:

"In fact, no civilization, not even that of ancient Greece, has ever undergone such a continuous and profound process of change as Western Europe has done during the last nine hundred years. It is impossible to explain this fact in purely economic terms by a materialistic interpretation of history. The principle of change has been a spiritual one and the progress of Western civilization is intimately related to the dynamic ethos of Western Christianity, which has gradually made Western man conscious of his moral responsibility and his duty to change the world. . . . The history of Christendom is the story of the progressive vindication of this tremendous claim which not only made the Church a far more dynamic social force than any other religious body that the world has known, but diffused its influence through the whole of Western civilization and affected spheres of thought and action far removed from the direct influence of religion."[1]

The second theme, that of the relationship of Christianity to the traditions of East and West, is presented in the introductory chapter to the present volume, "The Mediator Between East and West." The following passage is another expression of it. Showing the balance between Eastern and Western elements in the origin and development of the Christian tradition, Dawson writes:

"The Church itself, though it bears a Greek name, Ecclesia, derived from the Greek civic assembly, and is ordered by the Roman spirit of authority and law, is the successor and heir of an Oriental people, set apart from all the peoples of the earth to be the bearer of a divine mission.

"Similarly the mind of the Church, as expressed in the authoritative tradition of the teaching of the Fathers, is neither Eastern nor Western but universal. It is expressed in Western languages—in Greek and Latin—but it was in Africa and Asia rather than in Europe that it received its classical formulation. Greek theology was developed at Alexandria and Antioch and in Cappadocia, while Latin theology owes its terminology and its distinctive character to the African Fathers—Tertullian, Cyprian and above all St. Augustine."[2]

The third theme, the specific and unique character of Christianity, which sets it off from the Oriental world religions, is probably the most important, especially in the present age of proposed religious syncretism. Why is it that, so far as Christianity is concerned, the offer of religious syncretism must be rejected?

First, let us note some of the points of agreement between Christianity and the Oriental world religions. Dawson examines this agreement in chapters II and III of *Christianity and the New Age* (1931), later reprinted in part in *Dynamics of World History* as "The Stages of Mankind's Religious Experience." He writes:

"Thus each of the new religio-philosophic traditions— Brahmanism, Buddhism, Taoism, and Platonism— ultimately transcends philosophy and culminates in mysticism. They are not satisfied with the demonstration of the Absolute; they demand the experience of the Absolute also . . . .

"The whole religious experience of mankind—indeed, the very existence of religion itself—testifies, not only to a sense of the Transcendent, but to an appetite for the Transcendent that can only be satisfied by immediate contact—by a vision of the supreme Reality. It is the goal of the intellect as well as of the will . . . .

"Thus Christianity is in agreement with the great oriental religions and with Platonism in its goal of spiritual intuition, though it places the full realization of the goal at a further and higher stage of spiritual development than the rest. For all of them religion is not an affair of the emotions, but of the intelligence. Religious knowledge is the highest kind of knowledge, the end and coronation of the whole process of man's intellectual development."

If these are the points of agreement, what are the points of dissimilarity, the features that mark off Christianity as radically different from the Oriental world religions? In this same essay, we find the following distinction made:

"It may perhaps be objected that this view involves the identification of religion with mysticism, and that it would place a philosophy of intuition like that of the Vedanta higher than a religion of faith and supernatural revelation, like Christianity. In reality, however, the Christian insistence on the necessity of faith and revelation implies an even higher conception of transcendence than that of the oriental religions. Faith transcends the sphere of rational knowledge even more than metaphysical intuition, and brings the mind into close contact with super-intelligible reality. Yet faith also, at least when it is joined with spiritual intelligence, is itself a kind of obscure intuition—a foretaste of the unseen— and it also has its culmination in the spiritual experience by which these obscure spiritual realities are realized experimentally and intuitively."[3]

What this implies is that it is not man's own efforts and techniques which lead to an experience of union with God, but that everything depends on the graciousness of God and His decision to introduce man into the realm of supernatural

life. This lies beyond all human effort, and is attained only
by the gift of faith. As Dawson expresses this elsewhere,
"The life of faith is far wider and more intense than the activity of the pure intellect, which throws but a fitful and obscure light on the true nature of being." [4]

Moreover, it must be recognized that Christianity, unlike
the Oriental philosophic religions, does not exist in order to
provide for the attainment of mystical experience by the individual. Its purposes embrace the whole of humanity, and it
is therefore essentially historical in its orientation, rather
than mystical. The mystical experience is not denied, but it
is subordinated to the purposes of the historic Revelation. As
Dawson expresses this, after he has spoken of the mystic
flight of the Alone to the Alone:

"But this is not Christianity. Although Christianity does
not deny the religious value of contemplation or mystical experience, its essential nature is different. It is a religion of
Revelation, Incarnation, and Communion; a religion which
unites the human and the divine and sees in history the
manifestation of the divine purpose towards the human
race." [5]

Another way of comparing Christianity and the Eastern
world religions, both as to elements of agreement and of contrast, is given in the following passage from a letter by
Christopher Dawson to the present writer, in which Dawson
had been commenting upon the thesis of F.S.C. Northrop in
The Meeting of East and West:

"Now as I see it, the only basis for an understanding
between Christianity and the Eastern religions is on the

philosophic level. The Christian Platonist can converse with the Vedantist and the Mahayana Buddhist, and the Christian Aristotelian or Stoic can converse with the Confucianist. There is no room for a strictly *theological* understanding, because the theological component of the Eastern religions is just as lacking in truth and substance as is the theology of Greek paganism or as that of the religions of Canaan. Here no compromise is possible.

"Nevertheless there does remain the common basis of Natural Religion and Natural Law, which is the truth that underlies all the archaic cultures. I mean the idea of a divine order which is manifested on three planes, cosmological, moral and social, and in which the different planes are coordinated by the sacred ritual order of prayer and sacrifice. This is common to the Jew and the Gentile, to the Christian and the Confucian. But it is philosophical rather than theological, as we see in Hellenic culture, where this truth is expressed only by the philosophers—from the pre-Socratics down to the Stoics—and finds no clear expression in the current pagan religions of Greece and Italy.

"And the same is true of China, for when the early Jesuits tried to build on this consensus of Natural Theology, they were held up by the fact that while the Confucians were clear enough on the divine order, they had no real *theology*, no doctrine of God and of the Divine Nature.

"This is the fundamental idea in my theory of the World Religions. I stated it briefly in *Progress and Religion* and at full length in *Religion and Culture* [the first volume of Gifford Lectures [6]] . . . If this view is true, it is obviously all important for the history of the civilizations and the higher religions."[7]

When disciples of the Oriental philosophic religions recognize these facts, they then downgrade the significance of the personal element in religion—the worship of a personal deity or deities—making this out to be merely mythological and symbolic, and thus greatly inferior in value to the true reality which has been reached by religious philosophy. Dawson points this out in commenting on the thought of René Guenon, one of the more articulate disciples of Oriental religion in the period from the 1920's to the 1940's:

"This, however, is what M. Guenon refuses to recognize. To him religion is at best but a poor substitute for that true science of being which is the object of intellectual intuition, and therefore he regards Christianity as a diluted and impure form of that Oriental tradition which is to be seen in its higher form in the Vedanta. His point of view is, in fact, almost identical with that of Averroës, who places theology upon a lower plane than metaphysics. They are not contradictory, as the Western Averroists sometimes seem to suggest, for both sciences teach the same truths. In theology, however, these truths find a symbolic expression which renders them capable of assimilation by the mass of mankind, whereas in philosophy they are seen pure and unveiled in their essential reality."[8]

One may note the similarity of Guenon's approach to that of the demythologizers of the New Testament today, in which a particular existential kind of philosophy determines what truths of faith will be accepted. But whereas the Oriental popular religions are in fact dealing with mythological figures, not historical ones, and thus fit in with this kind of analysis, with Christianity this approach empties out its very substance. As a consequence of the mythological element in the Oriental religions, the objects of worship lend themselves quite readily to syncretism, along the same pattern as the gods of the ancient Mediterranean world who were brought together in the pantheon of the Roman Empire. And because of this fact, the different gods of Hinduism are prepared to accept in a context of syncretism the personal God of Christianity, Judaism, and Islam. Such a move leaves undisturbed the basic Oriental religious philosophy, which centers on an impersonal Absolute or an impersonal Law, rather than on a personal God. For Judaism, however, and for Christianity which has inherited the Jewish tradition, "There was one God and one Israel, and in the relations between these two was comprised the whole purpose of creation." Moreover, for the Christian, the fulfillment of that purpose was realized in the Incarnation of the only-begotten Son of God, who inaugurated a new order which would ultimately transform the whole of humanity. Dawson expresses the contrast of this belief with that of the Oriental religions, "And the source of the new order was found, not in a mythological figure, like the Saviour Gods of the Mystery Religions, nor in an abstract cosmic principle, but in the historical personality of Jesus, the crucified Nazarene." [9]

Consequently, offers of syncretism made by Oriental world religions as a means of resolving the differences between the Oriental religions and Christianity, are destructive of the very nature of the Christian Faith:

"On the one hand the religions of the Far East—Hinduism and Mahayana Buddhism—adapt themselves well enough to Dr. Toynbee's ideal of religious syncretism, but they do so by denying the significance of history and creating a dream world of cosmological and mythological fantasy in which aeons and universes succeed one another in dazzling confusion and where the unity of God and the historical personality of Buddha are lost in a cloud of mythological figures: Buddhas and Bodhisattvas, gods and saktis, demigods and spirits. On the other hand the three higher religions of the West—Judaism, Christianity, and Mohammedanism—have followed quite a different path. Their very existence is bound up with the historic reality of their founders, and with the establishment of a unique relation between the one God and His people.

"Thus any syncretism between religions of these two different types would inevitably mean the abdication of the monotheistic religions and their absorption by the pantheistic or polytheistic ones. Such a process is not inconceivable, but we have no historical reason to suppose that it is possible and no theological reason for supposing it to be desirable or right."[10]

The fourth theme, the opportunity which may exist for Christianity to become the religion of both East and West in a new cosmopolitan civilization, is dealt with in the next to last chapter of the present volume, "Christianity and the Oriental Cultures." Dawson sees the periods of intermingling of civilizations and cultures as the time when the opportunity is greatest for the widespread diffusion of a cultural tradition or a world religion. This was the situation, in fact, which allowed Christianity to spread so quickly and widely in the world of the Roman Empire; and it was a similar situation which favored the spread of Islam six centuries later. As to present circumstances with regard to the spread of Christianity, Dawson observes:

"Thus the Christian Church today and in the immediate future is confronted with a tremendous opportunity. The civilization of the new world has an immediate unsatisfied spiritual need. The Church has a universal spiritual mission, which she has hitherto been unable to fulfill because the nations have been separated from one another, speaking different spiritual languages, enclosed in separate worlds, each of which has been shut off from the rest by walls of custom and tradition. Now the old barriers that divided the nations have been broken down, and the sacred laws that ruled men's lives for thousands of years have lost their power. . . .

"But do we Christians today possess the power and the vision to carry out this apostolate in this new world that I have described? Although the opportunity is great, the difficulties are great also, and it will need great spiritual energy to overcome them." [11]

But it is just that spiritual energy which seems so greatly lacking among Christians in Western Europe and America today. The secularization of society has largely been accepted by Christians, who place their hopes more readily in economic goals and in secular ideologies than they do in the message of the Gospel. In fact, a kind of spiritual anemia has developed, which has had its effect in the loss of the moral dynamism which previously characterized Western society.

It is possible that there are parts of the Christian world where this religious malaise has not so deeply taken root. If such is the case, then these peoples will be the ones to carry forward the apostolate of the Christian mission to the nations of the East in the worldwide society which is now coming into being.

For such an effort, the universal significance of the Papacy, and its increasing impact upon the consciousness of peoples throughout the world, may well serve as a guiding light. For the Papacy stands today as a strikingly visible symbol of the spiritual influence of the Christian Church in a predominantly non-Christian world. In their prophetic witness against the evils which now threaten all of mankind, the popes have in fact assumed a supranational role. This transcends the barriers of religious and cultural divisions, which have for so long kept the peoples of the world apart. As Christopher Dawson has observed concerning this unifying role of the Catholic Church:

"In this dark world, divided against itself, cursed by the confusion of tongues and frustrated by the lack of common purpose, the Papacy speaks to the nations as the representative of the only power that can 'lead man back from the shadows into the light. The Church alone can make him conscious of the past, master of the present, and secure for the future.'

"The profound doctrine of the supra-national mission of the Church as the centre of spiritual unity in a divided humanity has been developed and taught by the Popes since the time of Leo XIII onwards. In our own day, we seem to see the beginnings of a new Pentecostal dispensation by which again 'all men hear in their own tongues the wonderful works of God.' The 20th century has been a catastrophic period, full of wars and the rumours of wars and the distress of nations, but it has also seen the dawn of a new hope for humanity. It foreshadows the birth of a new Christendom—a Society which is not confined as in the past to a single group of nations and a single civilization, but which is common to every people and language and unites all the members of the human family in the divine community of the Mystical Body of Christ."[12]

NOTES

1. *The Judgment of the Nations* (1942), pp. 23-24. (Reprinted by Howard Fertig, Inc. 80 East 11th St., New York, NY 10003.) For a brilliant exposition of the influence of Christianity on the development of science in Western culture, see Stanley L. Jaki's Gifford Lectures (1974-75 and 1975-76), *The Road of Science and the Ways to God* (Chicago: University of Chicago Press, 1978).

2. *The Historic Reality of Christian Culture: A Way to the Renewal of Human Life* (1960), pp. 116-117. (Reprinted by Greenwood Press, Inc., 51 Riverside Ave., Westport CT 06880.)

3. *Dynamics of World History*, pp. 178-180. (1958) (Republished by Sherwood Sugden & Company, 1117 Eighth St., La Salle, IL 61301. 1978. 510 pp. $7.95.)

4. "The Revolt of the East and the Catholic Tradition," p. 13, *The Dublin Review*, July, 1928.

5. *The Formation of Christendom* (1967), p. 18.

6. *Religion and Culture* (Gifford Lectures, 1947) (Reprinted by AMS Press, Inc., 56 East 13th St., New York, NY 10003.)

7. Enclosure with Christopher Dawson's letter of Nov. 5, 1954 to J.J.M.

8. "The Revolt of the East and the Catholic Tradition," cited in note 4, above.

9. *Progress and Religion* (1929), pp. 154-155. (Reprinted by Greenwood Press. Cited in note 2, above.)

10. *Dynamics of World History*, p. 398. (Cited in note 3, above.)

11. See Chapter 11 of the present volume.

12. See Chapter 12 of the present volume, "The Papacy and the Modern World."

Introduction:
The Mediator Between East and West

The signs of a nascent revolt against the European hegemony in the Orient were evident long before the First World War, but it was only in the decade following the war that the movement developed from the stage of subterranean agitation to the point at which it obtruded itself directly upon public attention. And undoubtedly the war itself was primarily responsible for the growth of unrest among the peoples of the Orient, not only because it weakened the military and economic foundations of European power, but still more on account of the moral disillusionment it produced, and the discredit that it threw upon the prestige of Western civilization.

Above all, the Russian Revolution and the propaganda against Western imperialism, which was organized by the Soviet Government and the allied communist organizations, gave unity and coherence to the activities of the various disaffected elements among the subject peoples and classes throughout the world.

Nevertheless, the movement of Oriental revolt against the

European hegemony is itself largely of Western inspiration. Its ideology is purely European, and owes nothing to the cultural tradition of the peoples whom it is seeking to free. Even in the literary sphere the leaders of Oriental thought, as conceived in Europe, are themselves men of Western culture and education. The central fact of the whole situation in East-West relations is not the relatively weak and superficial cult of Oriental ideas in the West, but the incomparably more powerful and far-reaching movement of Occidental ideas in the East.

During the years which followed the First World War, the traditional cultures of the East were shaken to their foundations. In Russia the Bolsheviks did their best to uproot Eastern Christianity, and to destroy the spiritual inheritance of the Russo-Byzantine tradition, turning the mind of the people towards the philosophy of materialism and the cult of the machine. In Turkey not only was the Caliphate abolished, but the religious law of Islam was abrogated, and the dress and manners of European civilization were enforced by law after the fashion of Peter the Great. Finally, in China, the sacred rites which had been the foundations of social and moral order for thousands of years were swept away, and the shibboleths of Western democracy took the place of the maxims of Confucius.

Hence the movement in the East that at first sight seemed to portend the downfall of European influence was in reality but another sign of the penetration of Asia by Western ideas and the defeat of the native Oriental traditions. This was not a temporary and superficial phenomenon, but marked the beginning of a new epoch in the history of the world.

To understand the significance of these developments for the future of Christianity in the East, certain facts must be taken into account. First, it should be recognized that the simple identification of Christendom and Western civilization can hardly be accepted, even for the past. The opposition of East and West is independent of Christianity, for it dates back to the pre-Christian era. Europe acquired her independence on the day when the navies of Greece and Asia fought in the Bay of Salamis under the eyes of the Great King, seated on his throne on Mount Aegaleos.

The theme of the feud between Europe and Asia runs through the whole of ancient literature, from the age of the "Father of History" down to the Augustan Age, And in his great description of the battle of Actium, Virgil sees the monstrous shapes of Oriental religion arrayed against the divine ideals of the Western soul.

Omnigenumque deum monstra et latrator Anubis
Contra Neptunem et Venerem contraque Minervam
Tela tenent.

Nevertheless it was the East that eventually conquered, and the conversion of the Empire to Christianity was the consecration of its victory. Christianity arose in the one province of the Empire that had preserved an undying hostility to the ideals of the Roman-Hellenistic culture and which preserved intact a purely Oriental tradition. It is true that the Oriental reaction was spreading through a thousand channels, some of which were far more fundamentally irreconcilable with the Western genius than was Christianity. Nevertheless the opponents of the new religion, from Marcus Aurelius and Celsus to Julian and Namatian, saw in it a dark Oriental superstition which threatened the very existence of Western culture. It may be that Hellenism was doomed in any case, and that the decline of the city state before the ideal of theocratic monarchy of the Oriental type was inevitable, but the change from paganism to Christianity was undoubtedly an essential aspect of the process which converted the Hellenistic into the Byzantine culture.

Some would perhaps point out that the Orientalism is peculiar to the Byzantine Church, and that it was the work of Western Catholicism to unite the Christian and the Latin traditions in a new cultural unity. But though this is to a great extent true, it does not exclude the intervention of Oriental influences. The centuries in which the Roman Church took up the burden of the Empire and advanced to the reconquest of the West after the barbaric invasions were at the same time an age in which the power of Orientalism was at its height.

Rome itself had become a Byzantine city, full of Greek monks and immigrants from the East. Syrian Caesars ruled at Constantinople, and the Holy See was occupied by a succession of Syrian and Oriental Pontiffs. It was a Syrian archbishop who was the organizer of the Anglo-Saxon Church; it was a Syrian pope to whom St. Wilfrid, the great champion of Roman authority, made his appeal; while St. Boniface received the pallium from another Syrian, St. Gregory III, and his legatine authority from a Greek, St.

Zacharias. Even the earliest monuments of English Catholicism are carved with the vine-scrolls and symbolic ornament of Oriental art.

Above all, the monastic institution, which may almost be called the parent of medieval culture, was itself of Eastern origin, and owed its existence to the naked, fasting ascetics of the Egyptian desert, in whom the Oriental ideal of spirituality finds its perfect embodiment. It is true that St. Benedict brought to the monastic institution a new element of order and moderation which may be regarded as essentially Latin. Nevertheless he did but adapt the Oriental tradition to Western needs and capacities, and the Middle Ages always looked back to the Fathers of the Desert as the purest examples of the monastic ideal. In the words of a medieval writer, the monks and solitaries "brought into the cold and darkness of the West the light of the East and the warmth of ancient Egypt."

All through the Middle Ages the civilization of Western Europe had its face turned to the East from which the light had come to it. The Crusades themselves were not so much a European offensive against Asia, as the result of the nostalgia of Christendom for the ancient cradleland of the Faith. Moreover, we must remember that the medieval line of division between the Christian and non-Christian lands did not coincide with that between Europe and Asia. The Baltic lands were still half pagan. Asia Minor and the Caucasus were largely Christian. Above all, the most highly civilized region of Western Europe, the Western Mediterranean basin, was the home of a strangely mixed culture in which

Catholicism, Judaism, Islam, and the Manichean sects all had a share. The Christian kings of Sicily and Castile were surrounded by Moslem and Jewish scholars and court officers; the Sultans of Andalusia and Morocco were served by Christian mercenaries and craftsmen. And this brilliant and heterogeneous culture was the natural intermediary between East and West. Through it Christian Europe received its chief knowledge of astronomy and mathematics, of medicine and alchemy; above all, of the Greek philosophers and their Arab interpreters. But these influences all ran in one direction. St. Thomas read Averroës, but there is no reason to suppose that Averroës had any knowledge of Anselm or Peter Lombard. Ibn Arabi influenced Ramon Lull, but the Moslem was too proud of his cultural superiority to learn anything from the young civilization of the West.

Thus medieval Christendom during its greatest period was permeated with Oriental influences. The religious opposition between Christianity and Islam coexisted with a certain cultural agreement. The Crusader and the Ghazi, the Cid and the Sidi, the Thomist and the Averroist met as enemies, but met upon a common ground. They maintained different doctrines, but they spoke the same intellectual tongue. The ultimate and unfathomable gulf which severed the Greek and Roman as well as the modern European from the Oriental had temporarily disappeared in the Middle Ages. Its reappearance was due to the same movement which destroyed the unity of Christendom and led to the secularization of the medieval culture. Ever since the Renaissance and the Reformation Western civilization has been separating itself from all dependence and contact with the East, and recovering the specifically Occidental characteristics of extroversion and material organization which had already marked the Graeco-Roman culture.

Among the peoples of Latin culture, the Catholic tradition was too deeply rooted to be replaced by a new religious doctrine. But while its supremacy in the strictly religious sphere was not challenged, it no longer dominated the whole culture. It was neglected and pushed on one side by the development of the new humanistic culture, the new scientific and philosophical ideas, and the new monarchy with its ideals of secular sovereignty and the preponderance of material interests. And this dualism finally ended in the complete victory of secularism, and the institution of a purely "lay" culture which tended towards the destruction of the spiritual power and the elimination of the last traces of religious influence.

In Northwestern Europe, however, the course of development was different. Here Catholicism was replaced by a new interpretation of Christianity which gave free scope to the development of the Occidental mentality. Protestantism eliminated all the Oriental elements in the Christian tradition. It abolished asceticism and monasticism. It subordinated contemplation to action, the spiritual to the temporal authority. Faith was no longer a human participation in the Divine knowledge, but a purely individual and nonrational experience—a man's conviction of his personal salvation. The Divine was no longer conceived as pure intelligence—*luce intellettual piena d'amore*—the principle of the intelligibility of the created universe, but as an absolute despotic power whose decrees predestined man to eternal misery or eternal bliss by the mere fiat of arbitrary will. And this divorce of intelligence from dogma led on eventually to an apparently contradictory conclusion—the dissolution of dogma in the interests of a moral pragamtism which is the hall-mark of much of modern Christianity. Christianity, it is said, is not a creed, it is a life; its sole criterion is the moral and social activity that it generates: and thus religion loses all contact with absolute truth and becomes merely an emotional justification for a certain standard of behaviour.

Thus the two movements that have dominated Western Europe since the sixteenth century, in spite of their difference of origin and mental atmosphere, have tended in a similar direction. Each of them has carried on the process of extroversion and the denial of absolute metaphysical principles to their logical conclusion by their several paths. Both of them have attained to the opposite pole of thought to that of the Oriental tradition, and equally both of them have arrived at the negation of Catholic ideas. Catholicism and Orientalism stand together against the denial of the higher intellect and of the primacy of the spiritual which is the fundamental Western error.

Nevertheless this is not the whole truth. If Christianity were entirely in conformity with the Oriental spirit, it would be difficult to explain the fact that it failed to maintain itself in its own Oriental homelands. For while Catholicism was advancing triumphantly to the conquest of the West, it was all the time fighting a rearguard action against the pressure of the forces of pure Orientalism, as represented by the Gnostic and Manichean sects, and by Islam. Against the Oriental religions of pure spirit which denied the value and even the reality of the material universe, the Church undeviatingly maintained its faith in an historical revelation which involved the consecration not only of humanity, but even of the body itself. This was the great stumbling-block to the Oriental mind, which readily accepted the idea of an avatar or of the theophany of a Divine aeon, but could not face the consequences of the Catholic doctrine of the Two Natures and the full humanity of the Logos made flesh. This conception of the Incarnation as the bridge between God and Man, the marriage of Heaven and Earth, and the channel through which the material world is spiritualized and brought back to unity, distinguishes Christianity from all the other Oriental religions, and involves a completely new attitude to life. Deliverance is to be obtained not by a sheer disregard of physical existence and a concentration of the higher intellect in the contemplation of pure being, but by a creative activity that affects every part of the composite nature of man.

The Oriental view leads to the depreciation of the normal human activity of the discursive reason, and to a contempt for all knowledge of the particular and for the humble but necessary discipline of physical science. The mind which withdraws itself to the heights of pure intelligence leaves the sensible world in the confusion of anarchy, for a practical irrationality is the Nemesis of speculative intellectualism. To the Catholic philosopher, on the other hand, the progressive intellectualization of the material world by reason and science is an essential function of the human mind. In the natural order man occupies a similar position as the bond of union between the spiritual and the material worlds, as that which he holds in the supernatural order by virtue of the Incarnation. The two are analogous and complementary.

Thus the Catholic Church appears Oriental to the West and Occidental to the East. She is a stranger in both camps, and her home is everywhere and nowhere, like Man himself, whose nature maintains a perilous balance between the sensible and intelligible world, to neither of which it altogether belongs. Yet by reason of this ambiguous position, the Catholic Church stands as the one mediator between East and West. She alone possesses a tradition which can satisfy both sides of man's nature, and which brings the transcendent reality of the divine Logos into relation with the tangible and visible facts of human experience.

1

The Relevance of European History

WORLD HISTORY, as it is understood today, is an entirely new subject. Sixty years ago, when Acton was planning the Cambridge Modern History, he conceived it as a universal history which would not be a mere combined history of modern states, but a study of the development of universal historical forces. Yet at the same time, he took for granted that this history would be a European one and that it was only, or primarily, in Europe and its colonies that the movement of world history was to be found. But the new conception of World History, as may be seen for example in the UNESCO world history which is being written at the present time, rejects this conception entirely and aspires to produce a work which will be ecumenical in treatment and scope, embracing the whole history of every people from China to Peru without preference or prejudice.

The old European view of history is now condemned as provincial or parochial or "ethnocentric," and it is generally admitted that if we wish to study world history we must pay as much attention to China and India and Islam, not to mention Indonesia and Africa, as to Europe.

At first sight this seems to represent a great advance, but even if this is so, the advance has still to be made. For the great European historians of the past, like Ranke and Acton, were members of an international society of learning and they spoke to a wide audience who knew what they were talking about. Today world history has no such educated public. General historical knowledge has not kept pace with the advance of specialized studies.

And it is inevitable that this should be so, since the linguistic barriers to the study of oriental history are almost insurmountable at the present time, except for a small class of specialists. Thus there is a serious danger that the relative widening of the historical perspective to include the non-European civilizations may be accompanied by an absolute decline in the quality and standard of general European history.

Curiously enough it has been left to an Indian writer— "an unknown Indian," he calls himself, Nirad Chaudhuri— to point out how grave this danger is. He writes as follows:

"In the last few decades there has certainly been seen in Europe, or at all events in England, a decline in historical knowledge, accompanied by a pronounced recoil from the historical attitude. This is a retrograde phenomenon, for if there is anything that distinguishes man from the other animals, it is memory or consciousness of duration, and I cannot understand how the European man, having attained the high degree of historical consciousness that he did in the nineteenth century, can have stepped back from it to the uncultured man's bondage to the present, and the still more uncultured man's bondage to the eschatology of political dogma. Yet what the European man is displaying more often than not today is an utter lack of the historical sense. I sometimes seek the solution of the puzzle in that Spenglerian vision, the dreadful and tragic *Untergang des Abendlandes,* the untimely decline of the European peoples on their home continent, brought about by an internal strife as insensate, as inescapable and as suicidal as that of the Greek cities. I ask myself: Are we witnessing a whole society's senile decay of memory?"[1]

This is a very severe judgment, but it is not altogether lacking in justification. It is borne out for instance by Professor Barraclough's recent volume, *History in a Changing World,* which is all the more instructive because it represents the views of a professional historian as offered to a popular audience. Now Professor Barraclough starts from the conviction that the Russian victory at Stalingrad makes a total revision of European history necessary, and he even goes on not only to discard the nineteenth-century conception of Europe as the centre of universal history, but to question the very existence of Europe as a cultural unity and of any real continuity between classical, medieval and modern history. "The European inheritance," he concludes, "is a tangle of unsolved contradictions, a thicket of dead ends, offering no direct line of advance" for the future. And so instead of the old Western tradition that is centred on Europe and Greece and Rome, he demands a "history that is truly universal—that looks beyond Europe and the West to humanity in all lands and ages." [2]

---

[1] *The Autobiography of an Unknown Indian* (New York, The Macmillan Company, 1951), p. 341.
[2] The Copp Clark Co., Ltd., Toronto.

Unfortunately, he does not explain how this new history is to be discovered. He does not even suggest where we are to begin. He only refers us to Herr Spengler's view of independent culture cycles and suggests that some new culture is going to arise in Russia or elsewhere—which will in time take the place of the defunct civilization of Europe.

But it would be a mistake to kick away the ladder of European historiography before we have found a foothold in the new world. The fact that Western Europe has lost its position of world leadership does not affect the significance of the European historical tradition. So instead of saying, Farewell to European History, as Alfred Weber and now Professor Barraclough have done, I would rather advocate a Return to European History, since I believe that it is only by way of Europe and the Western historical tradition that it is possible to approach that universal world history which has so long been the ideal of the philosophers of history.

Throughout the past, down to a century or two ago, the historic world was not an intelligible unity. It was made up of a number of independent civilizations, which were like separate worlds, each of them with its own historical tradition and its own idea of world history. During the last thousand years these great world civilizations have been four in number—China, India, Islam and Europe (or rather, Christendom, for the division between Western civilization and its great Eastern neighbours was always a religious rather than a geographical one).

It is true that the isolation of these four cultures was never complete. Europe was in contact with Islam, Islam was in contact with India and India was in contact with China.

But these contacts did not go very deep. In particular they did not extend to a knowledge of the other historical traditions, so that each civilization tended to ignore the historical pasts of the others. Moreover, these four civilizations were far from being world-wide. All together they represented an island of higher civilization in an ocean of darkness. And these barbarous outer lands were seen as lying outside the world of time as well as on the frontiers of the world of space. They were lands without history and even without common humanity.

Now the unique significance of Europe for the development of world history is to be found in the part that it has played in breaking down the isolation of the ancient world civilizations and bringing the unknown outer world into the light of civilization and history. This achievement is so momentous that there is nothing to be compared with it in human history since the original creation of higher civilization (which, however, preceded the dawn of history). Whatever is happening to Europe at the present time or may happen in the future cannot affect the significance of this world-changing event. It must, however, be admitted that modern European historiography has failed to do justice to it. Professor Barraclough is quite right in criticizing the disproportionate amount of attention that has been devoted to the political and diplomatic history of the Western European and North American States—to the English party system, to Frederick the Great and Bismarck and so on—as compared with the all-important question of the relation of Europe to the outer world. Here the nationalist and politicist bias of modern history has distracted attention from the epoch-making changes which have been Europe's real contribution to world history.

It is true that the field is overpoweringly wide and overruns all the conventional limits of conventional academic history. Economics, politics, religion, science and technology are all involved and all exercise a mutual influence on one another. The first step in this process—the breaking of the oceanic barriers of the Old World by the Portuguese and Spanish navigators—is no doubt familiar enough, and yet even here comparatively little study has been devoted to the social and economic background of the movement and to the problem of the continuity between the new forms of colonialism, and those which had already been developed by the Italian maritime republics in their establishments in the Black Sea and the Levant.

The second stage of the European world movement—the penetration of the closed world of the other old-world civilizations—was a much more gradual process, since it began earlier, in the thirteenth century, with the first great travels of the Friars and of Marco Polo to Central Asia, India and China, and has continued throughout the centuries ever since. Here it was the Christian missionaries who played the leading part, though the name of Marco Polo shows that the economic element was also present from the beginning. It was, however, the great missionaries like St. Francis Xavier, Matteo Ricci, Rodolfo Acquaviva, Robert de Nobili and the rest, who alike in India, China and Japan were the first to establish contact between East and West on the higher cultural level. Above all, the Jesuit mission to China in the seventeenth and early eighteenth centuries was unique for its double achievement in convincing Chinese scholars of the scientific values of European culture and in unveiling to Europe the whole extent of Chinese culture—its history, its literature and its institutions. And it is, I think, a legitimate criticism of our current methods of teaching history that for every hundred people who are familiar with the names of the geographical explorers like Tasman and Dampier and Bougainville there is hardly one who knows the names of the scholars who discovered Chinese culture like Ricci, Couplet, de Mailla and du Halde.

The only excuse for this is that the work of the great Jesuit missionaries and scholars belongs to the earlier phase of the European world expansion and did not lead on directly to the triumphant expansion of the third phase. The world hegemony of Western culture was introduced by the three great changes that took place during the eighteenth century—first, the Europeanization of Russia—the one province of Christendom that had remained isolated from the West from the time of the Mongol conquest down to the age of Alexis and Peter the Great; secondly, the establishment of an autonomous centre of Western culture outside Europe in North America; and thirdly, the British conquest of India. Owing to these developments the influence of European culture, which had hitherto been limited to the coasts and the islands, penetrated to the heart of the Asiatic and American continents and gradually subjected the trade and resources of the non-European world to the new Western economic and technical organization.

During the great age of Western capitalism in the nineteenth century, the whole world lay open to the enterprise

of the Western financier and merchant and to the skill of
the Western technician and engineer. All over the world
Europeans and Americans were prospecting for new sources
of wealth and opening up new markets and new channels
of trade. During its central period, from the time of Adam
Smith to that of Cobden and Bright, this economic movement was cosmopolitan rather than imperialist in spirit, and
was inspired by the ideals of the liberal Enlightenment. The
process which is now regarded as the exploitation of the
weaker peoples and classes by Western capitalism was seen
by contemporaries as the great means of world progress and
international peace. In the words of John Stuart Mill, "It
may be said without exaggeration that the great extent and
rapid increase of international trade, in being the principal
guarantee of the peace of the world, is the great permanent
security for the uninterrupted progress of the ideas, the institutions and the character of the human race." In the past,
"the patriot wished all countries weak, poor and ill-governed
except his own; now he sees in their wealth and progress a
direct source of wealth and progress to his own country."[3]

   And these ideas were not so absurd as they appear today.
So long as the economists and the politicians accepted the
Liberal ideology, they were more interested in the expansion
of trade than in territorial conquest, and the establishment
of a world-wide system of communications was regarded as
the common interest of all civilized peoples. As the Roman
road was at once the organ and the symbol of the Pax Ro-
mana, so the steamship, the railway and the telegraph were
the organs of the new pacific world unity which was the
ideal of the Western Liberal economists.

   [3] *The Principles of Political Economy* (ed. Ashley), 1909, p. 582.

Nor was this expansion of Western culture purely material. It involved the advance of knowledge and the communication of ideas—and that in both directions. Towards the end of the eighteenth century, Western science took up the work of the Jesuit missionaries and began to reveal an unknown world of oriental religion and philosophy. The discovery of Sanskrit literature (by Anquetil-Duperron, Sir William Jones, Sir Charles Wilkins and Henry Colebrooke) was one of the most epoch-making events of modern times. In the West, it prepared the way for an oriental renaissance which had a profound effect on European thought, especially in Germany and France, in the first decades of the nineteenth century. At the same time, in the East, the influence of Western ideas, combined with the European interest in Sanskrit studies, produced important changes in Indian culture. The spread of education, the development of the vernacular literatures, above all Bengali, and the influence of personalities like Ram Mohun Roy (1780–1833) and Debindra Nath Tagore prepared the way for the revival of Hindu culture and the growth of a new educated class and a new national spirit. Thus it was the West that created Indian nationalism by giving India a new sense of its cultural values and achievements.

This two-sided process of Western scientific study and oriental cultural awakening went on all over the East during the nineteenth century and has extended in the present century to the more primitive peoples of Africa and the Pacific. Here Europe achieved something that had never been done before, since neither the Greeks nor the Arabs nor the Persians, in spite of their interest in the manners and customs of strange peoples, ever succeeded in getting inside the

minds of the societies that they studied and comprehending
their culture as a living whole. Today this has become the
normal procedure of the modern social anthropology, but
its origins are much older than scientific anthropology, and
are to be found in the new oriental and historical studies.
Edward Lane's *Account of the Manners and Customs of the
Modern Egyptians,* published in 1836, is a classical type of
what I mean, though no doubt it is by no means the earliest
example. It seems to me to be closely related to the achievements of nineteenth-century historians—to works like de
Tocqueville's work on American democracy, on the one
hand, and to Fustel de Coulanges' book on the Ancient
City or Burckhardt's study of the Renaissance, on the other.

No doubt this new historical and sociological humanism
was the work of a small elite. For one man like Lane or
Mountstuart Elphinstone or Brian Hodgson, there were a
hundred Jos Sedleys or William Hickeys, and if there had
been more of the former type, the history of the modern
world would have been very different.

But, on the other hand, it may be argued that it was
Kipling's "Sons of Martha," the engineers and civil servants
and sanitary inspectors, who performed the essential task
of breaking through the inherited tyranny of prejudice and
custom and thrusting the new scientific and technical order
on a hundred unwilling peoples. It may be objected that this
function might have been performed by the oriental peoples
themselves without Western control. But Japan is the only
example of a people accepting a radical change in its way
of life without being forced to do so by Western economic
or political power. The natural reaction of oriental national-

ism to Western contact was reactionary in both senses of the word. Those reactionary nationalists or traditionalists who led the resistance to Western imperialism in the nineteenth century were by no means inferior in character to the leaders of the later nationalist movements—some of them, like 'Abd al Khadir in Algeria, Shamyl in the Caucasus, the Khalifa 'Abdullah in the Egyptian Sudan, were heroic figures, but they were doomed to inevitable defeat because they did not possess the techniques and the scientific organization of the civilization that they resisted. All the triumphs of modern oriental nationalism have been the work of men of Western education, who were able to use the ideas and knowledge of the West in the service of their own peoples.

This new class was, however, literary rather than scientific in training. It was composed, especially in India and in the Near East, of lawyers and journalists and schoolmasters, rather than engineers and doctors and economists. It remained for a long time suspended between two worlds—filled with enthusiasm for the material civilization and democratic ideals of the West, but still profoundly attached to the memory of its ancient cultural traditions.

Hence the ambivalence of the modern nationalist movements. The Westernized intelligentsia acted as the spearhead of national mass movements which were animated by anti-Western xenophobia. But the moment that independence had been secured, they took over the role of the European administrators and proceeded to modernize oriental society far more drastically than the old colonialism had ever dared to do. And this tendency is most pronounced in Communist states, where the traditional religious foundations of oriental

culture are being destroyed just as ruthlessly as the alien
power of Western capitalism, which is much less deeply
rooted. Thus the movement of world change that was inaugurated in Western Europe several centuries ago has now
been so fully assimilated by the East that it is being carried
forward by the very forces that are most overtly hostile to
the West. And though this may well mean the end of the
political predominance of Europe, it certainly cannot be
used as an argument against the significance of the Western
achievement. It is in fact a process which was foreseen and
foretold by some of the typical representatives of nineteenth-
century—and perhaps eighteenth-century—Liberalism, for
their idealism was cosmopolitan rather than nationalist in
its outlook. As Walt Whitman, the most aggressive booster
of the West, proclaimed, the great adventure of Western
Man, the discovery of the New World, is at the same time
a passage to India and more than India; the voyage of the
mind's return to its first wisdom—the understanding of the
past and the comprehension of the whole, and the meeting
of the two opposite poles of the globe in a united humanity.

This liberal idealism seems very remote from the racial
and cultural conflicts of the existing situation, not only in
Europe, but in Asia, Africa and the Middle East. Nevertheless we are witnessing far-reaching attempts to establish relations between Eastern and Western culture and to create
an organized system of world order, and both of these movements are the direct products of nineteenth-century Western
ideas. No doubt it is only too easy to conceive the breakdown of these attempts and the return by way of oriental
and African nationalism to a system of closed cultures. But

this offers no real prospect of a new creative culture cycle. Rather it suggests the coming of a new dark age and the gradual decline of the standards of culture. The only real alternative to the tradition of Western Liberalism is that of Eastern Communism, and this is so deeply committed to the principles of Western science and technology and to one version of Western social and political ideas that it can hardly be regarded as representative of oriental culture.

But neither can it be regarded as completely Western. It seems a kind of *tertium quid:* an intermediate power which stands in a somewhat similar position to the European state and to Western socialism as the reformed Tsardom of Peter the Great did to the Enlightened Monarchy of Europe in the eighteenth century. But in spite of the distance that Russian and oriental Communism has travelled from its Marxian origins in practice, it still remains completely faithful to the Marxian theory, and most of all in its theory of history. The Communist philosophy of history is still the original theory which Marx derived from his study of French politics, English economics and Hegelian metaphysics. And in spite of all the attempts that have been made to adjust this theory to non-European realities, the system still retains clear marks of its Western origin, being fully intelligible only when it is seen in its original nineteenth-century Western European setting.

No doubt it is possible to explain the development of Communism in different and non-Western terms. It might be seen as a reversion to the social and political traditions of the oriental state. After all, in Marx's own youth a very remarkable experiment in state capitalism was being carried

out in the Near East which in many respects foreshadows
the recent developments of state planning in Communist
countries. In the first half of the nineteenth century Mehemet Ali was carrying out a revolutionary reorganization
of the Egyptian national economy. The landlords were ex-
propriated, a new system of irrigation was introduced and
the peasants were compelled to cultivate new crops for the
export market. At the same time new industries were created
and state factories established. By 1830 it is said that ninety-
five per cent of the total exports and forty per cent of the
imports were on behalf of the state.

It is easy to see a parallel between this bold attempt to
collectivize and industrialize a peasant economy by direct
bureaucratic control, and what Stalin did in Russia under
his successive five-year plans; even the details are similar—
the resistance of the Kulaks, the sabotage of the new ma-
chines, the shortage of consumer goods and the sacrifice of
the peasants' standard of living to the requirements of the
state trading system. Certainly neither system has much in
common with the Marxian ideal of the workers' state, even
under the dictatorship of the proletariat.

But however true this may be, it is not recognized by the
Communists themselves. They are bound to remain faithful
in theory to the Western aspect of Communism, because it
is this element which gives the movement its popular appeal. For if Communism were seen as a return to the oriental tradition of state autocracy, if Stalin were regarded as a
Russian Mehemet Ali, it would no longer evoke the hopes of
the masses, since it would represent the cause of the oppres-
sor rather than the cause of the oppressed. The elements in
Marxism which are derived from the common tradition of

Western socialism and democracy—the appeal to justice, humanity and the rights of man, even though they are not realized in the totalitarian practice of the Communist state, are still absolutely essential to the success of Communist propaganda in the East no less than in the West; and thus Communism remains committed to Western social ideals.

So too with oriental nationalism. This also owes its moral appeal and its positive qualities to the political ideals it has acquired from the West. Modern nationalism is an exotic growth in Asia and Africa and its diffusion has followed closely on the spread of Western education. If it loses this leaven of Western ideals and becomes a negative xenophobic reaction against the West, it also becomes a destructive force. We saw this in India at the time of partition when the old mass loyalties asserted themselves in their naked elemental violence and the educated leaders of Indian nationalism recoiled in horror. But perhaps the most striking example of the strength of the Western element in oriental nationalism is the case of modern Turkey, where the Kemalist revival which arose in the hour of defeat to save the Turkish nation from external conquest ended by transforming Turkey into a modern secular state planned on strictly Western lines.

Thus it seems to me impossible to avoid the conclusion that the new Asia and Africa which are emerging with such revolutionary suddenness do not represent simply the reaction of Asiatic or African culture against the influence of an alien civilization, but rather the extension of Western civilization and Western international society into the extra-European world.

It is a process which may be compared with the move-

ment of national liberation in the Balkans during the nineteenth century, vastly different though it is in scale and
results. For the liberation of the Balkans did not mean a
return to the cultural traditions of their Byzantine past; it
meant the opening of the Balkans to Western civilization
and the gradual incorporation of the liberated nations into
the society of European peoples. It may be objected in the
case of Asia that this expansion of Western civilization was
the work of colonialism and that the destruction of colonialism is the *raison d'être* of oriental nationalism. Certainly
colonialism was the first stage of the process. As Karl Marx
wrote more than a century ago, in an article on India in
the *New York Times* of August 8th, 1853, England had to
annihilate the old Asiatic society before it was possible to
lay the material foundations of Western society in Asia. But
when once this function had been performed, colonialism
exercised a restrictive influence by protecting the institutions and interests which were rooted in the old order, as
we see in the case of the Indian Princes and client states.
The new order in Asia is the work of the new classes that
were created by Western education and Western economy,
and they have more in common with their opposite numbers
in Europe and America—professors and journalists and
industrialists and politicians—than with the priests and
princes and peasants who were the authentic representatives
of the tradition of Asiatic culture.

Alike in the Communist and non-Communist countries,
the chief problems that confront the new societies are educational and technological. They have to carry out with
great rapidity and on an enormous scale the changes which

were introduced slowly, step by step, in Europe and America in the course of centuries. Although they are all of them very conscious of the great traditions of oriental culture, they cannot look to these traditions for guidance in the work they have to do. Even in education, where the achievements of the ancient cultures were most remarkable, the break with the past has been almost complete. In India, Western education was firmly established long before the coming of independence, and though there has naturally been a reaction against the extreme occidentalism of nineteenth-century education, there has been no question of a return to Brahmin tradition. In China, on the other hand, the great tradition of Confucian education was still dominant in the nineteenth century, but it was the most formidable obstacle to the new ideas and therefore has been treated by the reformers as a reactionary force.

Thus alike in education, in technology and in economic policy, the peoples of Asia look to the modern West rather than to the ancient East for practical economic assistance and for theoretical, scientific and political principles: while at the same time their nationalism is based on an anti-colonial and anti-Western ideology which makes them intensely suspicious of Western political influence. And these two contradictory tendencies are the real explanation of the advance of Communism in Asia. Communism appeals to the peoples of Asia because it offers the alternative of a modern scientific technological order which is distinct from and opposed to the West as they have known it—to the old English and Dutch colonialism and to the new American business empire. Hence the non-Communist states are seriously

handicapped, since their nationalist ideology makes it difficult for them to co-operate with the West as wholeheartedly
as China can co-operate with the U.S.S.R., in spite of the
fact that the latter demands much more drastic changes in
the Asiatic way of life and in its religious traditions and
institutions. But whichever party triumphs, the invasion of
the East and of Africa by Western ideologies and technology
goes on without ceasing and the institutions and traditions
of the ancient cultures continue to decline.

It seems as though the whole world, East and West, were
moving by two different roads towards the same goal—towards a common world civilization, based on science, technology, social democracy and popular education.

But these two roads are very far apart from one another:
on the one hand the divided, many-branched ways of democratic nationalism, and on the other the straight, hard,
bloody highroad of Communist revolution; so that instead
of conducting the nations to a common goal, they seem to
be leading them apart to the destruction of civilization by
the intensification of ideological and communal conflict.

In this total world situation, Western Europe can no
longer hope to play a dominant political role, either for
good or evil, but Western civilization in its modern extension to America and Russia still remains the heart of the
conflict and the centre of modern world history.

And if we wish to understand the roots of the conflict
and the source of the revolutionary movements of change
that are transforming and possibly destroying the world, it
is to Europe in the traditional sense that we must look. As
the new science and technology are European in origin, so

also is it with the political and ideological conflicts of the present age. These conflicts were in their origin European ones, going back to the age of the French Revolution and to the party conflicts that divided Western socialists and liberal nationalists in the nineteenth century—to the days when Marx and Mazzini, Bakunin and Louis Blanc, Kossuth and Herzen all lived together in exile and waged their little ideological wars in London lodging houses. But today these conflicts are being fought out by Asiatic mass societies which know nothing of this cosy nineteenth-century background— societies which are neither bourgeois nor proletarian, and whose idea of nationality is founded on vast civilizations comparable to Europe or Christendom rather than to historic political unities like the Western European nations.

Nevertheless, the study of the European past is still relevant to modern world history, since Europe was the original source of the movement of change in which the whole world is now involved and it is in European history that we find the key to the understanding of the ideologies which divide the modern world. Indeed it must be admitted that historians themselves have a heavy share in the responsibility for the creation of these ideologies. No doubt it may be said that ideological history such as we find in Stalin's *Short History of the Communist Party,* or Rosenberg's *Myth of the Twentieth Century* is a grotesque caricature of true history. Nevertheless, such perversions would have been impossible if there had not been something seriously wrong with European history in the second half of the nineteenth century.

Modern nationalism would never have become so formidable if it had not been inflated by the genius of the great nineteenth-century national historians, and in the same way the Stalinist parody of socialist history could never have been possible without the work of Karl Marx, a man of genius whose real historical gifts were perverted and poisoned by his genius for hatred.

But there is no reason why history should always be used as the servant of ideological propaganda. It is time that we returned to the tradition of the great European orientalists and historians of whom I wrote earlier—men who were not concerned with political ideologies but with the patient investigation and interpretation of the thought and social institutions of other peoples. What we need is a new historical analysis of the whole process of world change, tracing the movement from West to East and taking account of the new factors which emerge at each stage in the process.

This process is so great that it transcends all the current ideological interpretations. It is not only an economic revolution in the Marxian sense, nor yet a process of colonial expansion on the part of the Western national states. It is the creation of a wider area of human communication which is coming to embrace the whole world. In order to understand it, we shall need, on the one hand, the help of the Western historians who can trace its origins in the European past, and on the other, the work of the orientalists who can appreciate the part of the non-European cultures and understand their reactions to the impact of modern civilization.

2

Renaissance and Reformation

THE period of modern history which extends from the Reformation to the French Revolution is a very difficult one to study and, I believe, there is a real danger that it may become increasingly neglected, especially by Catholic scholars. In the past and, indeed, until quite recently this period was regarded as "Modern History" and it was the main object of study not only by the popular literary historians, like Macaulay and Carlyle and Froude, but no less by the great men of learning, like Ranke and Acton, whose vast knowledge and powers of research have never been surpassed. But today Modern History has acquired a new meaning. More and more historians are devoting themselves to the study of the immediate past. New fields of study are being brought into the domain of history, while the wars and revolutions through which the world has passed in the present generation have changed our perspective and have made the Europe of the seventeenth century as remote as—and to Catholics, perhaps, more remote than—that of the thirteenth century. These centuries no longer belong to Modern History. Although they are not medieval in the technical sense, they are as it were a new middle age which separates modern Europe from medieval Christendom.

Nevertheless, though this period no longer belongs to "modern history," it still retains its importance since it is the age out of which modern Europe and the modern world have come. It is the age that saw the creation of the national state, the creation of modern science and the flowering of the modern vernacular literatures. Above all it is the age which saw the expansion of Western culture from its original West European centre to America and to the world. And it has a peculiar and tragic interest for Christians, because it was the age which saw the division of Christendom, when the Catholic and Protestant worlds assumed their existing forms and when Western culture began to undergo that process of secularization which has only been completed in our own days. If we do not understand this age, we cannot be said to understand European culture at all or American culture either.

Yet it is a very difficult age for us to understand; in some ways even more difficult than the Middle Ages proper. In the first place, we have always been taught to approach it from a strictly national standpoint. And though it is easy enough to study the England of the Tudors or the France of Louis XIV from this national angle, this makes it all the more difficult to study Europe as a whole. For then, as always, the typical European movements crossed the national frontiers and set up complex international relations which changed the national part as well as the European whole. The Renaissance, the Reformation, the Catholic Revival, the Enlightenment were all international movements, though each of them owed much to the leadership of some particular people. For while it is natural and right that we should study political history in terms of states or political units, it is also right that we should study civilization in terms of cultures.

In spite of the doubts of the positivist, a culture is just as much a sociological reality as a state. Indeed it is more real inasmuch as it has a larger social content. For it is at once a common way of life based on a common social tradition and also a spiritual community based on common beliefs and ideas. But while this conception of culture has become fundamental in the work of the modern anthropologist and pre-historian, it is still comparatively unfamiliar to the historian of modern Europe. And it is mainly on this account that the period of which I am speaking is so difficult to study, since, in spite of the immense wealth and variety of historical literature, there is a remarkable lack of standard works on European culture as a whole, especially during the seventeenth century when the Baroque culture of Catholic Europe transcended national and political frontiers as the culture of medieval Christendom had done.

This is particularly unfortunate because the age of which I am speaking began with two great international movements—the Renaissance and the Reformation—which had a profound effect on European culture and which cannot be explained in political or national terms. Neither can they be explained in terms of one another. In spite of the intimate and complex relations between them, both alike are aspects of the great cultural revolution which was due to the dissolution of the medieval unity of Western Christendom and to the reorganization of the different elements of Western culture according to new patterns. Throughout the medieval centuries from Charlemagne to the Council of Constance the unity of Western Christendom had been the basis of Western European culture. No doubt it is easy to exaggerate and to idealize this unity, but when everything has been said the fact remains that the Catholic Church was the mould in which all the diverse social elements of the Western society were brought together and fused into cultural unity. It gave the peoples of the West not only a common faith, but a common intellectual education, a common moral law, and a common system of organization. Technically the organization was an ecclesiastical one, but it entered into every aspect of social life and was in many ways stronger and more effective than the nascent political organization of the European state. For it was the Pope and not the Emperor who was the true head of Christendom, and he exercised a real superpolitical authority over the Kings and Princes of Western Europe.

Nevertheless, this Papal supremacy did not involve an Italian hegemony. The centre of the common culture lay north of the Alps in the area between the Rhine, the Rhone, and the Loire, and it was in this centre that the creative movements of medieval culture had their origin. In the eighth and ninth centuries it was the centre of the Carolingian empire and the Carolingian culture. In the tenth and eleventh centuries it was the source of the movement of monastic and ecclesiastical reform which had its centre in Lorraine and Burgundy, and it was the alliance of these two movements with the Papacy which determined the form of medieval Christendom and the character of its culture. So, too, in the following period this area was the source of the Crusading movement and of the Cistercian reform, and the centre of the university movement, of the scholastic philosophy and of Gothic architecture and art.

But the later Middle Ages saw the decline of all these movements except the last. Monasticism decayed, the Crusade was abandoned, the scholastic synthesis disintegrated under the influence of Nominalism, and the alliance between the Papacy and the movement of ecclesiastical reform was dissolved. And at the same time the focal area of medieval culture was divided and ruined by the destructive conflict of the Hundred Years War and the internecine feud between France and Burgundy. The Council of Constance represented a final effort of medieval Christendom to recover its lost unity. Thenceforth, the axis of Western culture shifted to the south.

In the Italian cities during the later Middle Ages, a new kind of society was being formed which differed radically from the feudal society of Northern Europe and tended to reproduce the old patterns of Mediterranean city culture. As the Northern culture centre declined, this revived Mediterranean culture grew in strength and self-confidence and became increasingly conscious of the great traditions of the past. This consciousness was increased by the fact that the Italian cities were now the dominant power in the Eastern Mediterranean and were thus brought into contact with a civilization older and more refined than that of continental Europe. For although the Byzantine Empire was moribund,

Byzantine culture was still a living force, and the beginning of the fifteenth century was even marked by a certain cultural revival inspired by Hellenic as distinct from Byzantine traditions. The centres of this revival were in European Greece, at Mistra in the Peloponnese, and at Athens, which was at that time the capital of a Florentine dynasty and the meeting place of Byzantine and Italian influences. Thus at the time of the Council of Florence (1439) the two movements of Italian and Greek culture were able to meet on equal terms, and the advent of Byzantine scholars, like Manuel Chrysoloras, Gemisthos Plethon, Demetrius Chalcondyles, Theodore Gaza, and Cardinal Bessarion stimulated the revival of Greek culture in Italy. Although nineteenth-century historians often interpret this movement as neo-pagan and hostile to the traditions of Christian culture, it was in fact regarded with favour by the Church, and its leaders throughout the Renaissance period held key positions in the Papal court and chancery. Indeed the alliance of the Papacy and the humanists was one of the dominant features of fifteenth-century culture and replaced the alliance between the Papacy and the monastic reformers which was characteristic of the eleventh and twelfth centuries.

Meanwhile in Northern Europe the preoccupation with the reform of the Church still persisted. But it was no longer associated with monasticism or with the Papacy. It tended rather to express itself in heretical or schismatic movements and to ally itself with the rising forces of nationalism and the national state as we see in the Hussite movement and even in that of Wycliffe which preceded it. Even the more orthodox reforming movement which expressed itself at the councils of Constance and Basel became increasingly hostile to the Papacy, so that at the very moment when Pope Eugenius IV and the Byzantine Emperor and patriarch had succeeded in ending the ancient schism between East and West, the West as represented by the Council of Basel was deposing the Pope and asserting the supremacy of the General Council against the Papacy.

It is true that the schism of Basel soon came to an inglorious end, but the neutrality manifested by Germany and so many of the northern princes showed how doubtful the allegiance of the West to the unity of Christendom had become. During the next seventy years the importance of the question of the reform of the Church was universally recognized, but no effective action was taken. The Papacy became increasingly absorbed in Italian politics while the northern rulers used the demand for reform as an excuse for extending their control over the Church in their dominions. Nor should we assume that the interest in reform was confined to the conciliar party or to Northern Europe. The Italians and even the humanists themselves were fully conscious of the need for reform. The greatest of the humanists, Pope Pius II, was also one of the last champions of the unity of medieval Christendom and the medieval idea of the Crusade, though at the same time he was well aware of the decline of these ideals and of the way in which national rivalries and political ambitions were destroying the unity of Christian society.

The European situation was ripe for an explosion. Martin Luther was simply the revolutionary leader whose passionate genius fired the train. He was the living embodiment of all the elements in Northern Europe which were most alien from Rome and from the new Mediterranean culture. He appealed from Hellenism to Hebraism, from Italian humanism to Northern religious emotion, from the authority of the Roman Papacy to the Christian Nobility of the German Nation. There was, however, one respect in which he agreed with the humanists: he shared their distaste for asceticism. The circumstances of his conversion caused him to react with extraordinary violence against the monastic life and the ascetic ideal on which it was founded, above all the ideal of virginity. And this was one of the most revolutionary aspects of his work, for the monks had been the makers of Western Christendom. They had dominated medieval culture from its beginnings down to the thirteenth century when their influence had been replaced by that of the friars, who represented the same ascetic ideal in a more popular and personal form.

Moreover monasticism was not peculiar to Western Christendom. It was common to the whole Christian world from Russia to Abyssinia, and to the whole Christian past since the fourth century, so that its destruction changed not only the social and institutional pattern of medieval culture but also the moral and spiritual ideals of the Christian life. Religion was secularized in the sense that it was reorientated from the cloister to the world and found its centre in the family and in the active fulfillment of man's earthly calling. No doubt all this was secondary in Luther's eyes to the fundamental evangelical doctrine of salvation by faith alone. But the destructive element of the Protestant revolution was more far-reaching than the positive, and was to some extent independent of it, as we see in the early history of the English Reformation.

For Henry VIII had no sympathy or understanding for Luther's religious ideas. The tradition to which he appealed was that of Philip le Bel and Louis of Bavaria, as we see from his publication of works like Marsilius' *Defensor Pacis* and the *dialogus inter Militem et Clericum* of which English translations were produced in 1533 and 1535. And so long as his schism followed these conservative lines it met with little resistance from clergy or people. But when from political and economic motives he followed the Protestant example and attacked the monasteries, the revolutionary character of his work became clear and it aroused a wave of popular Catholic feeling which under more vigorous leadership might have changed the course of history.

The Reformation was a revolutionary movement not merely on account of the excesses of fanatical minorities, like the Zwickau prophets or the Anabaptists of Münster, but because it changed both the spiritual and social order of the medieval world. Nothing is more remarkable than the rapidity with which the movement spread across the whole of northern Europe in the course of a few years from Switzerland to the Rhine to Scandinavia and the remote territories of Livonia and Courland. In these years the resistance of the Catholics was insignificant. The religious orders, notably the Augustinian Friars, were themselves the leaders of the revolt and before the Catholic forces had had time to rally, Germany had become three quarters Protestant and Scandinavia and the Baltic lands almost completely so. Only Iceland stood out for a little. When the first Icelandic monastery was destroyed by the Danes in 1539, the perpetrators were outlawed by the Althing and the governor was deposed. It was not until 1550 that the last Catholic bishop Jan Arason, the poet, was executed at Skalholt with his two sons.

But while it is impossible to exaggerate the importance of Luther as the source of the revolutionary movement which destroyed the unity of Christendom and split Europe asunder, his achievements as a constructor and organizer were relatively small and it is very doubtful whether Lutheranism would have withstood the Catholic reaction that followed if it had been left to its own resources. The wider development of Protestantism as a European movement which met the Catholic Counter Reformation on its own ground was mainly due to a genius of a very different type.

John Calvin was a French bourgeois, the son of a lawyer at Noyon, who brought to the service of the Protestant cause the logic and discipline and legal acuteness of the Latin mind. Unlike Luther he was essentially an intellectual, a scholar and a man of letters. But he was an intellectual who had the gift of ruling men, and from his study he was able at once to govern a state and to direct a world-wide movement of religious propaganda and ecclesiastical organization. In place of the somewhat shapeless and incoherent mass of doctrines and tendencies represented by Luther and the German reformers, he fashioned a coherent logical body of doctrine and an iron system of discipline, and in place of the state-controlled Lutheran territorial Churches, he created an autonomous Church which claimed theocratic authority. In this respect Calvinism inherited the tradition of the Catholic reforming movement of the Middle Ages, since it maintained the supremacy of the spiritual power as uncompromisingly as St. Gregory VII had done and was equally ready to resist any attempt on the part of the state to interfere in the government of the Church.

Thus in spite of the theological principles that were common to Lutheranism and Calvinism, their social appeal and their political effects were entirely different. Lutheranism had appealed to the princes and had transferred to the state the prerogatives and power and property which had belonged to the Church. Calvinism, on the other hand, appealed to the people, and especially to the newly educated middle classes, to which Calvin himself belonged. In the same way, while in Germany Protestantism soon lost the support of the humanists, so that Luther found his most formidable opponent in Erasmus, the leader of the intelligentsia, in France it was in humanist circles that the success of Calvinism was most pronounced, so that the leaders of Cisalpine humanism in the later sixteenth century, like J. J. Scaliger and Isaac Casaubon, were found among the Calvinists. In this way the Reformation in its second phase did a good deal to promote the cause of learning. The Calvinists, no less than their enemies, the Jesuits, fully realized the importance of education, and wherever they went, even as far as Massachusetts Bay, they brought not only the Bible but also the Latin Grammar.

Nevertheless this humanism was of a strictly utilitarian kind. Its adherents were the friends of education, but they were the enemies of culture and did their best to destroy and dissipate the wealth of religious art and imagery which had been accumulated by centuries of Christian culture. It was this fierce spirit of iconoclasm and the harsh intolerance that the Calvinists showed towards all the manifestations of Catholic piety which made any reconciliation between Protestantism and the movement of Catholic reform impossible and doomed Europe to more than a century of religious war and sectarian controversy.

The reaction to the tremendous changes brought about by Luther and Calvin also spread to the Mediterranean world. When Luther launched his revolt, the culture of humanist Italy had reached its maturity and Leo X, the son of Lorenzo de Medici, had made Rome the centre of a brilliant literary and artistic culture. Centuries later men looked back on the Rome of Leo X as a golden age. Voltaire writes of it as one of those rare moments in the history of the world which vindicate the greatness of the human mind and compensate the historian for the barren prospect of a thousand years of stupidity and barbarism. To Luther, on the other hand, the Rome of Leo X was a sink of iniquity, its culture was pure materialism, and its religion was gross superstition.

Neither of these extremes is justified. Leo X's generous patronage of culture cannot redeem his failures in his spiritual and international leadership. And the worldliness and moral laxity of Italian society do not prove that Italian religion was moribund. On the contrary its vitality is shown by the unbroken series of saints and mystics and reformers who flourished throughout the Renaissance period and who are to be found not only among the representatives of the medieval tradition like Savonarola but among the leaders of humanist culture. At Rome itself in the age of Leo X, the Oratory of Divine Love, out of which the Theatine Order arose a few years later, formed a centre of spiritual renewal which united leaders of the Catholic reform like St. Cajetan and Cardinal Carafa (afterwards Paul IV) with humanists and members of the Papal court, like Sadolet and Manetti, and later Reginald Pole, Aleander and Contarini.

The spirit of this Italian reforming movement was at once more medieval and more modern than that of the German Reformation. It aimed at applying the interior spirituality of the Italian mystical tradition—the spirit of St. Catherine of Genoa—to the task of ecclesiastical reform, and instead of revolting against the monastic and the ascetic traditions like Luther, it sought to adapt them to the needs of the age by providing a corporate quasi-monastic way of life in which the clergy could carry on their pastoral work, while living by rule in community. This innovation proved extraordinarily popular and successful. It exerted its influence not only by training priests and bishops but even more by providing an example which was to be followed by a series of similar institutions, the Barnabites of St. Antonio Maria Zaccaria, the Somaschi of St. Jerome Emiliani, above all the Roman Oratory of St. Philip Neri. It was this movement, even more than the Spanish Counter Reformation, which was the real source of the Catholic revival and of the new forms and ideals of modern Catholicism.

Nevertheless it did not possess the dynamic quality that was necessary to meet the challenge of the Reformation. The Christian humanists might have reason and authority and tradition on their side, but they were too civilized to cope with the titanic forces which had been released by Martin Luther.

But the Mediterranean world also possessed a new source of spiritual energy which was still intact. The rising force of nationality was making itself felt in the Iberian Peninsula no less than in Germany, but in Spain, unlike Germany, it was directed and unified by a strong central power. After centuries of division and strife the Spanish Kingdoms had been united in 1474 by the Catholic Kings who set themselves to reorganize and reform the whole national order, alike in Church and State. In this task they were able to appeal to the age-long tradition of the crusade against the infidel which had always been the dynamic force in Spanish history, so that they could unite their peoples externally by the reconquest of the remaining Moslem territories in Southern Spain and internally by the liquidation of the non-Christian minorities through the tribunal of the Inquisition, which was the organ of national unity as well as of Catholic orthodoxy and helped to identify the spirit of Spanish patriotism with Spanish religious ideals.

Hence the conquest of Granada in 1492, instead of marking the end of the Spanish crusade, only strengthened their sense of a national mission and transferred their crusading energy to new fields. At the same moment Spain became a great imperial power, owing first to the discovery of America, secondly to the conquest of Naples and finally to the union with Burgundy and Austria, which brought Spain into association with the Empire and hence into collision with the German Reformation. While the Flemish advisers of Charles V followed a policy of moderation and were not unsympathetic to Erasmus' conciliatory ideas, the Spaniards saw the religious conflict as the opportunity for a new crusade. As early as the Spring of 1521, the Council of Castille wrote to the Emperor, reminding him of the sacrifices which the Catholic Kings had made for the faith and begging him to call "the warlike and Christian Germans" to arms in order to seize Luther and send him a prisoner to Rome for the judgment of the Holy Father.

It was this Spanish crusading spirit which was to become the motive force of the Counter Reformation. By degrees it communicated itself to Charles V and his advisers so that eventually, and still more under his successor, the whole resources of the Spanish Empire were mobilized in a new holy war against European Protestantism.

Nevertheless this militant aggressiveness was only one aspect of Spanish Catholicism. Still more important was its internal spiritual mission for the reform of the Church and the restoration of Catholic culture, which found its expression in the work of St. Ignatius Loyola and the Society of Jesus. The beginnings of Ignatius were those of a spiritual Quixote, a knight errant in search of a crusade. But his retreat at Manresa, which coincided with that of Luther at the Wartburg, transformed his character and his aims and revealed to him his true mission, which was both internal and universal. The society which he created united the spirit of the Spanish Counter Reformation with that of the Italian movement of spiritual reform which was represented by the Theatines and later by the Oratory. Unlike the former it was essentially international in character and was directly dependent on the Papacy, but it also embodied the Spanish crusading ideal in a sublimated form, as we see above all in the heroic achievements of St. Francis Xavier, the apostle of the Indies.

No less important, however, in the long run was the activity of the Society of Jesus in education and culture. From the sixteenth century onwards the Jesuits set themselves to adapt the new methods of humanist education to Christian ideals, and their colleges, which were established all over the Catholic world from Peru to Russia, were the organs of a common type of humanist Catholic culture. Their work did more than anything else to restore the prestige of Catholic education, which had been so much damaged by the assaults of the humanists against the old scholastic tradition. And at the same time the work of the Jesuits as directors of conscience and spiritual advisers brought the influence of the Catholic revival to bear on the courts and cabinets, which were the key points of social influence and had hitherto been the centre of the disintegrating movements that had undermined the unity of Christendom.

But great as the contribution of the Society to the Catholic revival was, it was only a part of a much wider development. For example, the revival of the contemplative life and the new flowering of Christian mysticism, which was the spiritual climax of the whole movement, owed less to the Jesuits than to the Carmelite Reform, which arose slightly later and did not attain its full influence on the Catholic world until the early years of the seventeenth century. St. Teresa and St. John of the Cross, no less than St. Ignatius and St. Francis Xavier, are a proof of the extraordinary dynamism of the Spanish religious genius, and their achievement is even more representative of the Spanish religious tradition than that of the great Jesuits, since it is the culmination of a mystical tradition that was already flourishing, especially among the Spanish Franciscans, like Francisco of Ossuna, Bernardino of Laredo and St. Peter of Alcantara. Nevertheless it would be a mistake to ascribe the mystical revival of the sixteenth century entirely to Spanish sources. It had its independent roots in Italy, where one of the greatest of Catholic mystics, St. Catherine of Genoa (1447–1497), had had a profound influence on the spiritual life of Renaissance Italy through Christian humanists like Ettore Vernazza.

It is difficult to overestimate the share of the mystics in the Catholic revival and their influence on the new Catholic culture. The Protestant criticisms of Catholicism as a religion of external practices lost all their force when they were confronted with this new outpouring of divine grace and with the ideal of spiritual perfection manifested in the lives of the saints. At the same time mysticism provided the antidote against the rationalist and materialist tendencies in Western society and enlarged the range of humanist culture by a deeper and more sublime vision of spiritual reality, which inspired poets and artists as well as theologians and philosophers.

This too is an important factor in the Catholic revival, for the centres of the Catholic renaissance were also the centres of artistic production, so that Catholic art became one of the great channels for the diffusion of Catholic culture. Thus it is that the new Baroque art has given its name to the new culture which became the last great corporate

expression of Western religious ideals. For the expansion of
the Baroque culture was not merely an ideological movement, like the Enlightenment in the eighteenth century or
the diffusion of nineteenth-century Liberalism. It appealed
to the heart as well as the head and satisfied the emotional
as well as the intellectual needs of human nature. And thus
it was never merely the culture of an educated minority,
since its religious ideals embodied in painting and architecture and music were the common heritage of the people as
a whole and not the exclusive possession of a privileged
class.

Owing to this character, the Baroque culture possessed
exceptional powers of diffusion even among peoples of alien
traditions. On the whole, the modern expansion of European culture has been external and material. It has forced
non-European peoples to recognize the superiority of Western techniques and Western scientific knowledge, but it has
failed to bridge the spiritual gap between East and West.
But within the sphere of the Baroque culture this was not
so. Mexico and Peru and the Portuguese settlements in Asia
assimilated the Baroque culture and produced their own
local styles of Baroque art.

Thus by the seventeenth century Europe and the new
world were sharply divided between two apparently exclusive and antagonistic forms of culture. The Inquisition and
the ecclesiastical control of books and ideas, on the one
hand, and the penal laws against Catholicism, on the other,
seemed to create an impassable barrier which divided Catholic and Protestant Europe and America into two closed
worlds. How was it, under these circumstances, that the

unity of Western culture survived? Why did not the Baroque culture of Catholic Europe and the Protestant culture of the North go their own ways and gradually diverge further and further from one another until they became as mutually incomprehensible and as spiritually remote as Christendom and Islam?

The reason for this is to be found not so much in their common Christianity but in their common humanism. Both Catholic and Protestant Europe shared the same humanist education and the same classical literature, so that in spite of their spiritual separation they still maintained a certain community of intellectual life which prevented the divergence between Catholics and Protestants from completely destroying the unity of Western culture.

I do not go so far as to say that the humanist culture of the post-Reformation world was one and the same in every part of Europe. Religious differences had an even greater influence than national ones on its development, so that while Catholics and Protestants were alike influenced by their humanist education, it yielded different products in art and thought and life in different spiritual environments. Thus while humanism had as strong an influence on education and literature in Protestant Europe as in Catholic Europe it permeated the whole culture less deeply than it did the Baroque culture of the South. It produced great scholars like Scaliger and Casaubon and great poets like Milton, but it remained the culture of a minority. The educated classes had all undergone the discipline of humane letters, but the people as a whole derived their moral ideas and their spiritual imagery not from the philosophers or the humanists or the artists but directly from the Bible and above all from the Old Testament.

This Hebraistic tradition was characteristic of Protestant culture and has often been regarded, e.g. by Matthew Arnold, as responsible for the anti-humanist, Philistine character of middle-class culture in England and America. It was naturally strongest among the sects whose whole intellectual life was nourished on the Bible and the Bible only. But even in representatives of the highest Protestant culture, like Milton, there is a hard core of unassimilated Hebraism which is in conflict with their humanist education and which in lesser men produced a sharp dualism between religion and culture. It was this dualism which prevented the development of religious drama and religious art in the seventeenth century and caused that partial secularization of culture which destroyed the medieval unity of religious and social life.

In Catholic Europe, this was not so. As I have said, the Baroque culture was not confined to the scholars and the men of letters. It permeated the life of the people as a whole through the religious art and music and drama which continued to play the same part in the Baroque world as they had done in the Middle Ages.

Thus the drama instead of being banned by the Church was used deliberately as a means of religious instruction, so that in Spain, for example, religious and secular dramas were composed by the same authors, many of them priests, performed by the same actors and applauded by the same audiences. In the same way there was no sharp dualism in Catholic Europe between Christian and humanist ethics.

The synthesis of Catholic and Aristotelian ethics which was perhaps the most important of all the achievements of St. Thomas remained the basis of Catholic teaching and provided an ideal foundation for the creation of a Christian humanism which could integrate the moral values of the humanist tradition with the transcendent spiritual ends of Christian theology.

In Protestant Europe the influence of humanist ethics is considerable, as we can see in the Cambridge Platonists. Nevertheless the influence of the Old Testament was far stronger, especially in Calvinist countries, and it was this Hebraist ethos which explains both the strength and the weakness of Protestant culture. Alike in Calvin's Geneva and in Puritan New England, among Cromwell's Ironsides and among the Scottish Covenanters it produced a type of character and a way of life that were harsh and unattractive when judged by humanist standards but were as hard as iron and as irresistible as a steam hammer. This was the spiritual power behind the new economic order which was destined to transform Europe and the world. Against the rich communal life of Baroque Europe with its external magnificence and its internal poverty, its palaces and its monasteries, its saints and its beggars, there arose a society of godly merchants and shopkeepers and craftsmen who worked hard and spent little, who regarded themselves as God's elect, and who were ready to fight to the death against any attempt of king or bishop to interfere with their religion or their business.

No two forms of European culture could have been more different and more irreconcilable with one another. And yet both of them were intensely religious, and both alike were equally hostile, though in different ways, to the secularization of culture which was the dominant characteristic of the eighteenth century. In fact this process of secularization did not originate with either of them. It had its source in a third type of culture which was intermediate between the Baroque and the Calvinist worlds and which I shall discuss in the next chapter.

3

Rationalism and Revolution

WHEN one considers the progress of the Catholic revival in the sixteenth and seventeenth centuries and the apparent strength of religious faith and practice both in Catholic and Protestant Europe at that time, it is difficult to understand how European culture ever became secularized. In the middle of the seventeenth century Europe, and America also, were divided between opposing forms of religion and culture, but both of them—the Baroque culture of the South and the Protestant culture of the North—were intensely religious and sincerely Christian. Yet in a century or a century and a half all this was changed and Europe had become the Europe that we know. Religion had become a matter of private opinion and the public life of the state and the intellectual community of culture had become almost completely secularized.

This change was even more revolutionary than that of the sixteenth century, although it was less spectacular. For it was not the result of the French Revolution. The spiritual revolution had been already accomplished before there was any question of a political one.

How then are we to explain so vast a change? It was not, as is sometimes supposed, the direct consequence of the Reformation, nor was it due to the political or cultural victory of the Protestant North over the Catholic South. Yet on the other hand its had no roots within the Baroque culture itself, for the latter had attained a state of social and political equilibrium which might have endured for centuries, if it had not been disturbed from without. Spain and Italy were as impervious to Protestantism as Scotland and Scandinavia were impervious to Catholicism. And so too in America there was no possibility of mutual influence or understanding between the Protestants of New England and the Catholics of New France or New Spain.

But to this rule there was one great exception. Throughout the decisive period in which the new Catholic and Protestant cultures were becoming stabilized, the largest national state in Western Europe remained divided between the two religions. The French religious wars of the sixteenth century had ended in a kind of stalemate by which the leader of the Protestants became the representative of French national unity by himself becoming a Catholic, while at the same time guaranteeing the rights and privileges of the Protestant minority. The Edict of Nantes not only secured freedom of conscience for the Protestants; it recognized their corporate existence as an organized society—a state within a state—with their own religious and political assemblies, their own fortresses and practically their own army.

Nevertheless these very generous terms did not represent a Protestant triumph, but rather a victory for the party of conciliation, the so-called Politiques, who were prepared to sacrifice the principle of religious unity to the cause of national unity and who found their leader and representative in Henry IV himself, who repeatedly changed his religion according to political circumstances; once insincerely in order to save his life after the massacre of St. Bartholomew and once with apparent sincerity at the moment when his conversion gave him the crown and defeated the European hegemony of Spanish Catholicism.

For Henry IV the re-establishment of national unity after forty years of civil war was the first essential. If his subjects were good Frenchmen they could be Catholic or Protestant, but they must be Frenchmen first. And this point of view made a strong appeal to a generation which had been ruined by the miseries of civil war, deafened by religious controversy and touched in their national pride by foreign intervention. They welcomed the restoration of the royal power as an impartial arbiter which would be strong enough to impose peace on the rival Churches and parties which were tearing France in pieces. It is true that the age of Henry IV and Richelieu witnessed a great movement of Catholic revival which produced a galaxy of saints and mystics, like the Spanish revival in the previous century. But unlike the latter it was not a universal movement which embraced and inspired the whole culture, but a minority movement, which like the Puritan movement in England was a protest against the secularizing tendencies of the national culture. This analogy with Puritanism is especially visible on the left wing of the French Catholic revival which is represented by the Jansenist movement and which contributed no less than Protestantism itself to the loss of religious unity and to the growth of a sectarian spirit.

Meanwhile the work of Henry IV was being carried on

by Cardinal Richelieu, the classical representative of the *raison d'état,* who did more than Gustavus Adolphus or Cromwell to defeat the international policy of the Counter Reformation and to destroy the political unity of Catholic Europe. And this ruthless system of international power-politics which established the greatness of France on the ruin of Central Europe went hand in hand with an equally ruthless system of internal centralization which prepared the way for the absolute national monarchy of Louis XIV.

The effects of this revolution were not only political; they were also religious and cultural. The Gallican Church became more and more an autonomous ecclesiastical organism and French culture became progressively detached from the Baroque culture of Catholic Europe. This new national culture still shared the ideals of the humanist culture, but instead of applying them, as the Baroque society had done, to the service of an international religion, it used culture, in the Augustan manner, as an instrument of government and empire. This ideal found its most complete expression in the palace of Versailles and the elaborate ritual of the court of Louis XIV. All the resources of the nation were concentrated on the worship of the Roi Soleil whose splendour in turn was reflected by every facet of French culture. As Racine himself said in one of his discourses to the Academy, "All the words of the language, and even the syllables, seem precious to us because we regard them as so many instruments with which to serve the glory of our august protector."

Accordingly literature and art were subjected to a strict social regime, administered by the various royal academies: the Academie Française, the Academie des Sciences, the

Academie des Beaux Arts, and the rest. There was no longer any room for the unbridled fantasy and spiritual ecstasy of the Baroque genius. The watch-words of the new culture were order and regularity, good taste and good sense, reason and clear ideas. Its spirit was essentially classical but it was also rationalist, and this rationalist element gradually permeated the whole culture until it undermined and ultimately destroyed the authoritarian orthodoxy of the Gallican Church and the authoritarian absolutism of the French monarchy.

The source of this rationalist tradition was, however, quite distinct from that of the academic classical culture. For at the same time that Richelieu was reorganizing the political and social order according to the principle of the *raison d'état,* another great man, Descartes, was reorganizing the world of thought according to abstract mathematical principles. He was essentially a revolutionary genius who made a clean sweep of authority and tradition and created a new intellectual world by the unaided powers of individual reason. And yet there was a profound affinity—and even a spiritual identity—between the rationalism of this most independent of thinkers who lived in voluntary exile in Holland and the spirit of the new classical culture. So that in spite of the opposition of all the vested interests in the Church and the Universities, the Cartesian movement won the support not only of the scientific world but of all the leaders of French culture and French religion with the partial exception of Pascal—whether they were Gallicans like Bossuet, Jansenists like Arnauld and Nicole, or mystics like Malebranche.

Nevertheless the transcendental ontological aspect of Descartes' philosophy, which explains its religious appeal, was not the element that was the most influential or the most enduring. As Fontenelle wrote, it was not the metaphysics of Descartes but his new method of reasoning that was the important thing. The ordinary educated man for whom Fontenelle was the spokesman could make nothing of Malebranche's "vision of all things in God" or even of Descartes' proof of the necessity for the Divine existence, but he was very sensible of the value of clear ideas and of the importance of submitting received opinions and beliefs to strict rational criticism. There is, after all, a democratic and anti-authoritarian principle explicit in the new Cartesian method. Does he not begin his discourse by asserting that "Good sense is of all things in the world the most widely distributed" and that "good sense is by nature equal in all men"? And it was this universal appeal not to the trained intelligence of the philosopher but to the good sense of the ordinary man that was the great characteristic of the eighteenth century when the French classical culture and the new "philosophic" ideas were alike diffused from one end of Europe to the other through the cosmopolitan society of the courts and the salons.

Nor was this development confined to Catholic Europe, for a parallel movement was taking place in England, which destroyed the religious unity of Protestant culture and prepared the way for its secularization. In England as in France the nation had gone through a period of civil and religious strife which had made men look for some principle of unity that stood outside the field of theological controversy. As the religious wars in France had discredited both the Hugue-nots and the Catholic League, so the English Civil Wars had discredited the intransigence both of the Puritans and of their Episcopalian opponents. But in England, unlike France, the monarchy itself had been defeated. Strafford, who might have been the English Richelieu, had lost his head. So too had Charles I, and though the act of regicide had shocked the popular conscience, it dealt a blow to the doctrine of Divine Right from which the English monarchy never entirely recovered. Henceforth the English people sought a middle way which it found, after a very unrevolu-tionary Revolution, in a regime of limited monarchy and limited religious toleration combined with unlimited indi-vidualism and freedom of thought.

This English solution was exactly the opposite to that of France, and the two nations were involved for twenty-seven years in almost continuous war. Yet in spite of their national and political differences both English and French culture show a similar reaction against mysticism and religious "en-thusiasm" and a similar trend towards science and ration-alism.

It is true that there is a sharp contrast between the geo-metrical reason of Descartes and the empirical common sense of Locke, which reflects the difference in spirit of the two cultures. Nevertheless these two schools of thought met and mingled with one another in the culture of the Enlight-enment. The philosophy of Voltaire and the Encyclopaedists was that of Locke rather than of Descartes. Yet the driving force behind it is still the Cartesian rationalism with its sub-lime confidence in the infallibility of reason, its dissolvent criticism of received beliefs and traditions, and its determination "never to accept anything for true which I did not clearly know to be such."

Thus the spiritual barrier which divided the two post-Reformation cultures of Catholic and Protestant Europe was broken down, not by the victory of one over the other but by the weakening of religious convictions before the self-confident, superficial rationalism of the new lay intelligentsia.

Other factors besides philosophical ones contributed to the breaking down of the cultural frontier between the Catholic and Protestant worlds at the close of the seventeenth century. Above all the Revocation of the Edict of Nantes and the expulsion or forcible conversion of the French Protestants had the opposite effect to that which Louis XIV intended. For the Protestant exiles who swarmed into Holland and England in their thousands acted at once as the disseminators of French culture and as propagandists for the cause of religious toleration and political liberty. There has never been a body of *emigrés* so intellectually active and so socially influential as the Huguenot exiles. In England they provided the translators, like Abel Boyer, Des Maiseaux, Pierre Coste, Peter Motteux, and the rest, who acted as intermediaries between English and Continental culture. In Holland, which was the chief centre of the emigration, they became the founders of international journalism, and the French reviews and encyclopaedias which poured from the Dutch printing presses had an enormous influence on European opinion. The famous Dictionary which was published by the greatest of these Huguenot publicists, Pierre Bayle, in

1695–7 was more widely read than any work of the kind. It became the freethinker's vade mecum and prepared the way for the work of Voltaire and the Encyclopaedists. Moreover, it must not be forgotten that the Huguenot exiles still possessed a large body of secret sympathizers inside France among the ex-Protestants and crypto-Protestants who had become nominally Catholic under the stress of persecution. It is, of course, difficult to determine the exact influence of this factor in the secularization of French culture, since in the nature of the case it was a subterranean and to some extent an unconscious influence, but it was certainly of considerable importance owing to the position that the Protestant middle classes had held in economics and professional life. In any case, it was largely owing to the work of the French Protestant exiles that the new secular culture acquired a cosmopolitan character. This culture was still French in spirit and ideals, but it was no longer identified, as in the seventeenth century, with the power of the French monarchy and the political expansion of French power.

Nevertheless it was still limited to the three northwestern countries—France, Holland and England—with a somewhat uneven extension into north and west Germany. The Baroque culture of southern and central Europe still remained a closed world, and owing to the authoritarian character of the governments and the control of the Church over education and literature, the new culture and the new ideas had little opportunity of infiltration.

But it so happened that at this moment at the turn of the century a great change took place on the political level which entirely altered the balance of European culture. The extinction of the Hapsburg dynasty in Spain and the War of the Spanish Succession suddenly brought Spain and Spanish America under the rule of the Bourbons and broke the connection between Spain and Austria which had played an important part in the history of the Counter Reformation and the rise of the Baroque culture.

At first sight it may seem surprising that a mere change of dynasty should have any deep effect on a nation that was so jealous of its independence and so fiercely attached to its national and religious traditions as Spain. But though the spirit of the people was unchanged, the Spanish government in the later seventeenth century was in a state of such extreme disorder and impotence as to create a vacuum in the centre of the political organism. Into this vacuum there came a foreign dynasty and a new government which were naturally French in sympathy and were forced to rely on the power and prestige of Louis XIV in order to establish themselves.

Thus the eighteenth century in Spain was characterized by the predominance of foreign influences. The Spanish court became a satellite of Versailles, like so many European courts of the period, and the way was open for the penetration of new men, new manners and new ideas into the very centre of national life. The result was a breach in the continuity of Spanish culture which led to the divorce of Spain from her old connections with Austria and Baroque Europe and which incorporated her artificially and externally in the new international society of French culture with which she had no organic historical relation. The Spanish people remained faithful to their old spiritual ideals and cultural traditions, but these could no longer influence the course of history as they lacked intellectual and political leadership. Thus there arose that dualism between the Gallicized culture of the ruling classes and the traditional culture of the common people which was to endure for two centuries and which produced such catastrophic results in later history. The classical French culture of the *Grand Siècle* and still more that of the eighteenth-century Enlightenment had neither sympathy nor understanding for the ideals of the Baroque culture, and this antipathy led to a general depreciation of Spanish achievements and traditions which gradually infected the mind of the educated classes in Spain itself and produced that sense of inferiority which became characteristic of the *afrancesados* and liberals of the later eighteenth and early nineteenth centuries.

Nor is this surprising when we consider the changes that had taken place in Spain's international position. In the world of the Baroque culture Spain had always possessed a pre-eminent position, not merely on account of her political power but owing to the spiritual prestige of her saints and mystics and theologians. But in the new culture of the Enlightenment these spiritual achievements counted for nothing and less than nothing. Spanish culture had to start afresh as a backward pupil of the philosophers and economists whose whole scale of values contradicted that on which Spain's former greatness had been founded.

The extent to which this disavowal of the past went is to be seen in the part which Spain took in the destruction of the Society of Jesus (1767)—the event which marks the end of the great period of modern Catholic culture which had begun at the Council of Trent. Even in France the destruction of the Society (1764) was an act of political irresponsibility which was contrary to the true interests of the French monarchy. But in Spain it was much more than this: it was a suicidal act which ran counter to the whole national tradition and destroyed the keystone of the common spiritual culture which had formerly united Spain with Baroque Europe and which still united Spain with her colonial Empire.

Meanwhile in central Europe the Baroque culture still remained alive and active. Indeed the last decades of the seventeenth century and the first half of the eighteenth century were the great age of the Austrian Baroque. This was the age that saw the reconquest of Hungary and Croatia from the Turks, the final defeat of the advance of Islam into eastern Europe and the re-Catholicizing of the Danubian lands under Leopold II and Charles VI. It was also the golden age of German Baroque art, when the great monasteries and pilgrimage churches of architects like the Dietzenhofers, Prandauer, Fischer von Erlach, Baltasar Neumann and Dominikus Zimmerman were arising all over central Europe. If religious art and architecture and music are any indication, there can be no question of the vitality of Austro-German Catholic culture in the eighteenth century. Nevertheless this culture was the final product of a European movement which was already a thing of the past, and it could not survive the loss of its international background.

Consequently in the second half of the eighteenth century it came to an abrupt end, and Germany accepted the Enlightenment as suddenly and completely as she had accepted the Reformation two centuries earlier.

The transformation of German culture was due to a double movement which operated simultaneously from without and from within, from above and from below. (1) On the one hand, there was the direct influence of the French Enlightenment which acted through the courts and the rulers, like Frederick II of Prussia and Joseph II of Austria; (2) on the other, there was the awakening of German Protestant culture which created a new literature and a new philosophy. It was this, far more than any political change, which made the German middle classes conscious of their national unity and of their social importance, and this new spirit of cultural nationalism was transmitted not only to Catholic South Germany, but also to the non-German peoples of the East, like the Czechs and the Magyars, who had hitherto shared in the international unity of Baroque culture which was Latin rather than German in origin.

It was this combination of rational enlightenment and romantic nationalism which broke down the traditional order of Church and State in both Catholic and Protestant Europe and caused the complete secularization of Western culture.

The leaders of the Enlightenment were fully conscious of the revolutionary character of their work, and all through the middle decades of the eighteenth century they were carrying on a regular campaign of propaganda which was primarily directed against the Catholic Church as the archenemy of the Enlightenment.

In 1765 Voltaire wrote to Helvetius: "Do you not see that

the whole of Northern Europe is on our side and that sooner or later the base fanatics of the South must be confounded? The Empress of Russia, the King of Poland, the King of Prussia, conqueror of superstitious Austria, and many other princes have raised the banner of philosophy. During the last twelve years there has been a perceptible revolution in men's minds. . . . The light is certainly spreading in all directions." (Voltaire, *Lettres* VI:X)

No doubt Voltaire neither foresaw nor desired the revolution that was actually to come. He even says in the letter I have just quoted: "I well know that the established hierarchy will not be destroyed, for the people needs one." Nevertheless the destructive criticisms of the philosophers had undermined the order of Christian culture more completely than they realized, and it only needed the coming of a dynamic emotional impulse which appealed to the masses for the revolution to become a social and political reality. This element was supplied by Rousseau and his disciples, who found in the democratic ideology of *the rights of man* and the *national will* a new faith strong enough to inspire a new social and political order.

The theories of Rousseau had the same relation to the ideology of the Jacobin party as the theories of Karl Marx to the ideology of communism. Indeed there is a genetic relation between them, since the history of the modern revolutionary movement has been a continuous one, so that democracy, nationalism, socialism and communism are all of them successive or simultaneous aspects of the same process. Thus there is a socialist element in the thought of a typical nationalist like Fichte, a democratic element in Marx and a nationalist element in Stalin.

In the same way we can see in all these movements, with the partial exception of nationalism, the influence of the eighteenth-century Enlightenment. This continuity with eighteenth-century ideas is to be seen most clearly in the case of European Liberalism, which is simply the continuation of the Enlightenment in the nineteenth century and its adaptation to the conditions of capitalist society. But socialism and communism have also remained faithful in their fashion to the belief in human progress and perfectibility and in the boundless powers of human reason and science which characterized the eighteenth century. Marx himself regarded the philosophical achievement of the Enlightenment as no less important than the political achievement of the Revolution and goes so far as to say that even developed communism derives directly from French eighteenth-century materialism.

How is this ideological view of the European revolution to be reconciled with the economic interpretation of history? In Marx's view the intellectual and the political revolution were essentially one and both were based on the economic revolution and the rise of bourgeois capitalism. And the attention of Marx was so concentrated on this last factor, especially in its industrial phase, that he tended to ignore or underestimate all the factors which did not square with his theory. Nevertheless, to anyone who studies the history of the process as a whole, it is obvious that throughout the greater part of Europe the intellectual and religious changes which produced the secularization of Western culture preceded the economic revolution and were not produced by it.

In Germany and throughout Eastern Europe, as well as in Italy and Spain, the agents of change were not the new capitalist *bourgeoisie* but the old professional middle class, the men of letters and the professors, the lawyers and the government officials. Even in France, where economic conditions were more advanced, the capitalists who played a part in the Enlightenment were not the industrial capitalists but chiefly the "Farmers General" and the government contractors who represented a tradition as ancient as the *publicani* of the Roman Republic.

As in Russia so in Europe generally it was the intelligentsia, the class to which Marx himself belonged, and not the capitalists or the proletariat who were the real agents of change and the source of the revolutionary tradition.

The other essential factor was the political organization which these classes served—*the State:* not the popular state of the democratic ideology, but the new model of centralized absolutism which had been created by Richelieu and Louis XIV (or rather his ministers) and which had been imitated and developed by the "enlightened despots" of the following century—Peter the Great and Frederick the Great and Catherine the Great and their followers.

This affinity and collaboration between an "enlightened" intelligentsia and an enlightened despotism still persists in the Marxian tradition of the revolutionary intelligentsia and the revolutionary dictatorship, and today it has reached its ultimate conclusion in the totalitarian absolutism of Soviet Communism in which the police state and the ideological party have become fused with one another and where every aspect of culture is submitted to a process of strict psychological conditioning and control in the interest of a dogmatic secularist ideology. But today this movement is no longer a characteristically Western and European one. More and more it is passing over to Asia and becoming identified with the reaction of oriental nationalism against Western predominance and European culture.

Under these conditions what are the prospects of Western culture? It is impossible to go any further on the road of revolution and secularism which has been followed for so long, for this road has reached its ultimate conclusion. Only two alternatives remain. We can either remain in the half-way house of liberal democracy, striving desperately to maintain the higher standards of economic life which are the main justification of our secularized culture; or we can return to the tradition on which Europe was founded and set about the immense task of the restoration of Christian culture.

However difficult this task may seem to be, it is not an impossible one, for the most difficult part of it has already been accomplished: the almost miraculous survival of Christianity in a secularized culture. Two hundred years ago Christian culture was in a state of extreme decadence which affected the life of the Church itself and for which there seemed to be no human remedy. The destruction of the Society of Jesus by the action of the Catholic monarchies and the confirmation of their work by the Papacy itself marked not only the defeat of Catholicism as an international force but the self-acceptance of that defeat; and the subsequent action of the Revolution in the dechristianization of France and the secularization of the European order was only the logical completion of this process. But from that moment the tide began to turn. In comparison with the eighteenth century, the nineteenth century was an age of Catholic revival, which witnessed the restoration of the religious orders, the revival of Christian education and Christian philosophy and a new expansion of missionary activity. Above all the Church reasserted its independence of the State and became more than ever before a completely autonomous and unified international society.

Now if all this was achieved against the spirit of the age, in face of the triumphant progress of secular civilization, it should surely be far easier to carry the process of restoration a stage further into the sphere of culture and social life, at a time when the hopes of secular progress have been so bitterly disappointed.

At the same time we must not forget that the Catholic revival of the nineteenth century was rendered possible by the survival of a living Christian tradition among the masses, whereas today secularism has penetrated deeply into the popular consciousness. The problem that we are facing today is therefore quite unlike that which confronted the Church in the post-Reformation period. Our position is more like that of the Christians under the Roman Empire, when the Church had on the one hand to convert the pagan masses in the great Mediterranean cities, Antioch and Ephesus and Rome, and at the same time to defend its bare right to exist against the crushing weight of an all-powerful world state which recognized no limits to its authority.

4

The Missionary Expansion of Western Christendom

THE position of Christianity in the world today has been rarely considered by modern historians. It is none the less a question of central importance for the understanding of modern civilization. For twelve centuries Christianity has been the religion of a culture—that is to say, it has had an organic relation with the social and moral structure of one particular society of peoples. It has held somewhat the same place in Europe that Islam has held in Western Asia, Hinduism in India, or Confucianism in China. It has been the official creed of Western man; it has moulded his institutions, ruled his education and either created or influenced his moral values and his spiritual ideals. During the last two centuries the bonds of this organic union have been loosened and modern civilization has been progressively detached from its religious roots. Yet at the same time this has not involved the disappearance of Christianity as a living religion—on the contrary, these centuries have witnessed a remarkable expansion of Christianity throughout the world, an expansion which is partly due to direct missionary activity and partly to the extension of Western civilization across the Atlantic and the colonization of the empty spaces of the world by peoples of European stock and Christian tradition.

What is the significance of this twofold and apparently contradictory process? Is this modern expansion of Christianity merely the religious aspect of the world hegemony achieved by Western civilization in the eighteenth and nineteenth centuries? Or does it portend the advent of a new and truly world-wide Christendom in which Christianity will achieve a new organic relation with the world civilization of the future?

There is much to be said for each of these alternatives, but hitherto the question has never been adequately discussed. In particular, there have been few attempts to study the expansion of Christianity in the last one hundred and fifty years, apart from Professor Latourette's massive seven-volume *History of the Expansion of Christianity*.

First of all we must recognize the ambivalent character of the nineteenth century. This period has seldom been regarded as a great religious age, and has more often been viewed as an irreligious century, the age which saw the passing of the old order in Church and State and the birth of the new scientific and industrial civilization. Yet there are some, like Professor Latourette, who take a very different point of view. For them the nineteenth century was preeminently an age of hope and unlimited opportunity for spiritual as well as material achievement. And it is certainly true that it has only been in the last century and a half that Christianity, for the first time in its history, transcended the limits of a particular culture and became a world-wide movement which reached every continent, and almost every people and language.

In the nineteenth century this expansion was very closely linked with the colonial and economic expansion of the Western peoples—so closely that it has often been regarded as the same process in a religious form. In the present century, however, under the impact of the new non-occidental nationalist movements, the connection between Christianity and the expansion of the West has been weakened. The leadership in the missionary Churches is passing from the foreigner to the native element. But at the same time the advance of Christianity has continued with increasing intensity. In the last thirty years the percentage of Christians among non-occidental peoples has been doubled or more than doubled in spite of the fact that the new political and social movements which have been characteristic of the age have been unfriendly or openly hostile to the Christian faith.

This in itself is a remarkable achievement, and at first sight it seems to justify the optimism with which some Christians face the prospect of the decline of the West. But it is as yet too soon to say whether the Christian penetration of the non-European world is profound or superficial. Our views on this question will depend on our view of the nineteenth-century development from which it sprang. And the degree of one's optimism will be especially determined by the judgment one passes on the specifically "Anglo-Saxon" type of Christianity which contributed so much materially, morally and culturally, to the great movement of expansion of missionary activity in the last one hundred and fifty years.

It is truly an astonishing record. The religion of the old

world, and especially the sectarian Christianity of the British Isles, was sown broadcast in the virgin soil of America, and produced new varieties which in turn were propagated round the world till they came back to Europe once more. The Schwenkfeldians, "the Confessors of the Glory of Christ," have vanished from their native Silesia and survive in Pennsylvania, while there are still disciples of the English prophetess Mother Anne Lee who maintain their strict community life in the State of Maine. On the other hand, the Seventh Day Adventists, who appeared as a tiny sect in New England in the middle of the nineteenth century, have expanded steadily in all directions, from China to Peru, until by the middle of this century they had reached two hundred and ninety-five lands and five hundred and four languages. And the same intense missionary activity is shown by the other sects of American origin, such as the Mormons, the Christian Scientists and the body that is known as "Jehovah's Witnesses."

No doubt none of these bodies is representative of the main tradition of American Christianity. All, however, possess the missionary impulse and the power of expansion which is lacking in some of the more classical types of American Protestantism, notably in the case of the Unitarians, the Church of William Ellery Channing and Emerson, which has made such a considerable contribution to American religion and life.

In reading the history of the geographical expansion of Christianity, we cannot be satisfied with quantitative standards. At every stage we are faced with the problem of quality, with the nature of the religion which is diffused and the character of the men who are diffusing it. At every stage we must ask, what was it that spread? By what processes did it spread? What effect did it have on its new environment and vice versa? And why has the process of expansion sometimes been arrested or reversed? But it is not easy to answer these questions. Indeed nowhere is the apparent irrationality of history more apparent than in this field. Why was the Church of Cyprian and Augustine extinguished in North Africa, while the Church of Abyssinia survives to this day? Why did the Pitcairn Islanders become Seventh Day Adventists, and the Tonga Islanders Wesleyans? Why have the flourishing Nestorian Churches of Eastern Asia disappeared except in Malabar, where it is no longer Nestorian but Monophysite? These are historical accidents, like the survival of Buddhism in the Nogai Steppes in Russia or the Albanian Uniats of Southern Italy.

But we need some deeper and more universal cause to explain the steady westward trend of Christianity and the fact that the great modern expansion has been almost solely by its two Western forms, Roman Catholic and Protestant. For it is at first sight most surprising that the reaction of oriental nationalism against the West has brought no expansion to the Eastern forms of Christianity; it is from the Western Missions, and especially those of America, that the new Christendom of the Far East and of Africa is derived. Sun Yat-sen was the pupil of the Anglicans. The Soong family and Chiang Kai-shek were Methodists of the American denomination. Even in Japan, where the conflict with the West has been sharpest in the past; where the government had done all in its power to incorporate the Christians into the totalitarian national community before the collapse of the Japanese Empire in 1945; the influence of Western Christianity remained strong, and Toyohiko Kagawa, who was an outstanding figure in the Christian national movement, was characteristically Western in his religious approach to the social problem.

No doubt this expansion of Western Christianity owed much to the political and economic expansion of Western civilization. But this is not the whole explanation. It was due even more to the inner vitality of the forces of Christianity which had found a new social expression in the changed environment of the new world. In the English-speaking world during the last two centuries Christianity has been free to develop in its own way by its own resources without state control or political interference. In other words, the pattern of Church and State as fixed by the legislators of the later Roman Empire and the Carolingians was replaced by a new type of voluntary organization which has provided the pattern for the new Churches of the new non-European world. Yet at the same time there was no complete break with the past, and the Churches of America remained in full communion with their parent Churches of the old world.

At first sight this development seemed to mark the victory of the Protestant over the Catholic type of Christianity. But, as the nineteenth century proceeded, it was seen that this was not the case, and in the twentieth century it became clear that the Catholic Church was not only able to adapt itself to the new pattern, but actually derived fresh strength and energy from the changed conditions. This is shown most strikingly in the United States themselves, where Catholicism began as the unpopular religion of a minute and unprivileged alien minority and where it has grown until it is by far the largest and most powerful of the American denominations, numbering far more than the combined total of the Congregationalists, the Episcopalians and the Presbyterians, who between them represent the older traditions of American religion.

A similar situation is to be found in the Far East, Australia and Africa, where the absence of state support seems to stimulate rather than check the advance of Christianity. Here also the nineteenth century was the great age of Protestant expansion, while in the twentieth century the advance of Catholicism has been even more rapid. And the result has been that, as Professor Latourette remarks, "For the first time in its history Christianity was becoming really worldwide and not a colonial or imperial extension, ecclesiastically speaking, of an Occidental faith. Indeed in this it was unique. No other religion has ever achieved such world-embracing dimensions. We may go farther and say that no set of ideas, not even the widely propagated Communism of the period, had ever been so extensively represented by organized groups or so rooted among so many different peoples."[1]

This advance of Christianity into new fields has, however, been accompanied by a recession in Christendom itself, where the old type of a society that was traditionally and culturally Christian has been destroyed or threatened by the

[1] *History of the Expansion of Christianity* (New York, Harper and Brothers), vol. vii, p. 411.

rise of the totalitarian state and the drastic secularization of society and culture. The overt persecution of religion in Communist Russia and, in the past, in Nazi Germany, may be a transitory phenomenon, but the tendency to the secularization of culture is continuous and universal and there is no sign of any return to the ideal of a positive Christian culture, such as Mr. T. S. Eliot has described in his *Idea of a Christian Society*. Everywhere Christians, whether Orthodox, Roman Catholic or Protestant, are tending to be self-conscious minorities set in an alien or hostile world.

This trend has been undoubtedly strengthened by the catastrophic events of the last few decades which have shown how fragile is the barrier which separates the highest material civilization from the lowest depths of destructiveness and inhumanity. Already in the years between the two world wars there was a strong tendency to reject the liberal optimism of nineteenth-century Protestantism in favor of the uncompromising Barthian theology of crisis which has had such a wide influence on religious thought both in Europe and America. This tendency has been even more accentuated by the destructive effects of World War II and the threat of atomic warfare which now hangs over the world. The result has been to discredit, in some degree at least, that alliance of the forces of religious idealism and humanitarian reform which contributed so much to Protestant missionary activity from the time of Wilberforce and Buxton to that of the Christian Student Movement and the Universal Christian Council for Life and Work. At the same time the field of voluntary social activity has been restricted, and in some cases completely closed, by the extension of state action and the determination of the totalitarian socialist and nationalist parties to control every possible channel of social influence. This determination of the modern secularist, either to confine the Church to the sacristy or to use it as the obedient servant of the totalitarian state, threatens the freedom of Christian life to a degree in which it has never been threatened before.

The problems involved by this new situation have as yet not been fully realized by public opinion, except in reference to some particular conflict. Yet it is clear that even though National Socialism has been destroyed and Communism seems to have adopted a new policy towards religion, these problems will remain, and must have a profound effect on the expansion of Christianity. It is too soon to say whether they will produce a major recession of Christianity which will counterbalance the gains of the last century and a half, or whether they point towards a situation like that of the early centuries of our era, when Christianity first developed its world mission as a vigorous and persecuted underground movement.

It is impossible to give a confident answer to these questions, for the forces that are involved are too unpredictable and mysterious. Nevertheless, if one's personal sympathies are with the new voluntary type of missionary Christianity, rather than with the traditional European pattern of hereditary Christian culture, the prospect of a shifting of the centre of gravity from Europe to the non-European world will not seem an alternative greatly to be feared. And there are, moreover, new grounds of hope for the Protestant in the trend towards unity which during the last fifty years has increasingly taken the place of the fissiparous tendency which for centuries seemed inseparable from Protestantism, most of all perhaps in the United States. It seems, in fact, as though the sectarian principle had worked itself out, and that a new form of ecclesiastical unity is being gradually built up in the Protestant world. This movement has taken two forms. In the first place there has been the creation of United Protestant Churches, such as the United Church of Canada formed in 1925 by the coming together of the Methodists, the Congregationalists and the Presbyterians, the Church of Christ in China, constituted in 1927, and the Church of Christ in Japan, in 1941. In the second place there is the Ecumenical Movement, which is federal and co-operative in spirit and world-wide in scope and which has found its organ in the World Council of the Churches.

No doubt there is a wide difference of opinion with regard to the importance of this movement. There are some who see in it a sign of flagging energies and a decline of the religious individualism which sprouted so vigorously in a hundred sects. Nor is there any sign that it is likely to bridge the gap between Protestant and Catholic Christianity, and to bring the whole Christian world into a single religious community. Some leaders of the World Council look forward rather to the development of two world-wide Christian societies, organized not against one another, but against a godless and secularist world. Certainly the rise of the Ecumenical Movement has not increased the antagonism between Catholicism and Protestantism, which is actually strongest in those sects which have held most aloof from it. Nevertheless the conception of a world Christianity permanently and consciously organized on a dualistic basis is one which is obviously unsatisfactory from many points of view—most of all from its incompatibility with the fundamental Christian concept of the one Body, the importance of which is realized today by every school of theological thought more clearly than at any time in the past.

Everywhere we are witnessing a return to corporate ways of thought and action, a new realization of the religious significance of the community and an increasing interest in the expression of collective consciousnness in myth and ritual and art. This marks a great change from the individualism of nineteenth-century civilization, which characterized Westtern religion as well as secular culture, above all in Britain and America.

The great missionary expansion of the nineteenth century was everywhere based on the principle of individual conversion, and this is equally true of the internal development of Western religion which, as we see in all the most characteristic religious documents of the period, was marked by an introspective psychological approach and an intensely personal view of conversion and salvation. There is a fundamental contrast between this approach and the collective or communal form of expression which had dominated the Christian world for upwards of a thousand years. Western Christendom was not built up by the method of individual conversions. It was a way of life which the people accepted as a whole, often by the decision of their rulers, and which when accepted affected the whole life of society by the change of their institutions and laws. It is easy to condemn this type of corporate Christianity as superficial, external or subchristian, but at least it means that Christianity is accepted as a social fact which affects every side of life and not merely as an opinion or a specialized group activity or even as a hobby. Nor can we assume that the kings and bishops who laid the foundations of Western Christendom were less in earnest or less genuinely Christian than the leaders of modern sectarian Christianity. If the former shared the weakness of the barbarian culture from which they sprang, the latter have often been no less affected by the influence of the commercial and competitive civilization in which they lived. Moreover it may well be claimed that the missionary Churches of the Dark Ages produced a richer harvest even in the sphere of culture than anything that the modern missionary movement can show. There is little in the new non-occidental Christianity that can be compared with Bede and Boniface, with the religious art of Northumbria or with the new vernacular Christian literature. For in the case of Anglo-Saxon England, the mass conversion of the people meant the rebirth of culture, whereas too often the modern system of individual and competitive conversion has involved the piecemeal disintegration of native culture. There is surely something to be said for the view of the anthropologists who believe that every culture, even the most primitive, has a right to exist, and that a way of life which has been slowly and painfully evolved by a particular people to meet the needs of its particular environment has a value and significance for that people which nothing else can supply. If such a people is suddenly and completely transformed by their translation into an entirely different cultural world, they stand to lose more than they gain.

On the other hand, the alternative of protecting the culture of the simpler peoples from violent disruption while introducing them gradually into a wider moral and spiritual community has much to commend it. For it preserves the true essence of cultural nationalism, which is the instinctive loyalty that every people feels for its traditional cultural values, while subordinating it to the universal moral values which are the essence of a higher civilization.

The instantaneous switch-over from the total isolation of primitive barbarism to total integration in the modern world-society imposes an unbearable strain alike on human nature and on the way of life of a simple society. There must be an intermediate stage of education and acclimatization, and this stage is provided by the Christian missions better than by the nationalistic movements which promise too much and give too little.

It is true that modern missionaries are becoming increasingly conscious of their responsibilities in this respect, and are making a positive effort to avoid the disruption of native culture and to adapt their teaching to the indigenous forms of thought and social structure. But this is a very recent movement which is part of that return to corporate ways of thought to which we have just referred. In some cases, as in Polynesia and many parts of Africa, it has come too late to prevent the disintegration of culture, while elsewhere it is in danger of being overwhelmed by the rising tide of oriental nationalism which is apt to regard Christian missions as a form of Western imperialism. It is obvious that the new nationalism, with its superpolitical implications, must tend to strengthen the resistance of the oriental religions to Christianity regarded as a Western religion, and to missionaries as disseminators of Western culture. This tendency is strongest in India and in the Moslem world, where religion and culture are so closely linked that they seem to form an inseparable whole. It is less pronounced in China and Japan, where the relation of religion and culture are not so close, and where the situation is complicated by the competing claims of Communism, which is also a missionary movement. Everywhere, however, conditions are becoming adverse to the spirit of free religious enterprise which founded missions and schools and hospitals, supported by foreign contributions and staffed by foreign workers. The days of free trade in ideas are over.

The ideological character of oriental nationalism, like that of the totalitarian parties, makes it impossible to treat education or religion as neutral territory which can be left open to the free activity of independent religious organizations. Hence we are returning to a situation similar to that which existed in the Middle Ages, where men's beliefs are no longer a question of individual choice but of mass decisions.

The totalitarian ideologies advance today, as Islam did in the early Middle Ages, by a combination of military conquest and ideological propaganda. And Christianity is forced to face this challenge, not because it has a political character or seeks political power, but because the new ideologies seek to conquer and occupy the whole ground of community life, psychological as well as sociological. One should not identify Christianity simply with the traditional culture of Western Christendom, for it is the nature of

Christianity to transcend culture as it transcends nationality. But the sectarian Christianity of the nineteenth century avoided the difficulty because it was subcultural and unaware of the spiritual implications of culture, rather than because it was supercultural and able to embrace all peoples in the catholicity of a supranational bond of Faith.

5

The Spread of Western Ideologies

THE four great civilizations which constituted the world that we know were all spiritual communities that owed their unity to a common religion. In China, India, Islam and Christendom alike, political citizenship and racial origins were secondary to religious belief and practice. The Indian who ceased to observe the laws of caste and the worship of the gods and accepted the teaching of Mohammed ceased to be a Hindu and became a Moslem. And, in the same way, the western Moslem who became a Christian did not merely change his religion; he passed over from one civilization to another and acquired rights of citizenship in a new society.

During the last two centuries this situation has gradually changed. Nationality has taken the place of religion as the ultimate principle of social organization, and ideology has taken the place of theology as the creator of social ideals and the guide of public opinion. All over the world, beginning in Western Europe and extending gradually to the most remote regions of Asia and Africa, a change has taken place in the conditions of human existence and in the ways of social thought. The world has been made one, first by European trade, conquest and colonization, and later by Western science and technology. And behind the railway, the motor lorry and the airplane, there has spread a wave of secular ideas which had their origins in Europe in the age of the Enlightenment of the French Revolution, and which have communicated the ideas of political liberty and social equality, of nationality and self-determination from one people to another until they have become literally world-wide.

Although these ideas all had a common origin, during the nineteenth century they became differentiated into a number of distinct ideologies which were regarded as mutually exclusive and tended to become embodied in political parties and regimes. Thus Liberalism and Nationalism, Democracy and Socialism, Communism and Fascism all acquired this ideological form, although they were rarely found in a pure state. For example, we find National Liberalism and National Socialism in Germany, Liberal Democracy and Social Democracy in France and other similar compounds in other countries. At the present time there is a tendency for Liberal Democracy of the American type and Communist Socialism of the Russian type to become the opposite poles round which all the other ideologies and political regimes range themselves.

Thus we have two distinct ideological complexes, Western Democracy and Eastern Soviet Communism, which threaten to divide the world between them. Both of them are European, and even Western European in origin, but neither of them has its centre in Europe; one is Eurasian and the other is Euramerican. Both of them are secular ideologies as contrasted with the religious ideologies on which the four ancient world civilizations were based. Yet neither of them is entirely secular; Western Democracy is tending more and more to regard itself as the ally and protector of religion, while Soviet Communism, in spite of its avowedly anti-religious character, has always owed much of its success to its quasi-religious appeal. This is especially true in Asia, where Communism appears in the guise of a new religious or social way of salvation which promises to liberate men from oppression and suffering, on condition that they accept its authority and discipline by an act of unconditional surrender and obedience.

How does Europe stand in the face of this situation? Its position differs from both that of America and that of Asia. America has grown up with the new ideology. It can hardly conceive of a society which is not secular and democratic, since this is the only society it has known. In Asia, on the other hand, the movement of secularization is very recent and very alien to the traditions of Asiatic culture; indeed, it was only with the coming of Communism that the secular ideologies reached the masses and imparted a revolutionary momentum to the movement of social change. Even today in India, and even more in the Islamic world, the life of the people is still governed by religious beliefs and practices rather than by the secular ideologies.

In Europe, the ideologies are a native growth and have exercised a profound influence on European culture for at least two centuries. Nevertheless they have never completely destroyed the older tradition of Western Christendom, to which Europe owed its existence and its original sense of spiritual and cultural unity, and these two elements still exist today in a state of unstable equilibrium and tension. On the

Continent, Christian opinion has become organized through political parties and social programmes in the ideological pattern, so that it is sometimes regarded as one of the rival ideologies. In England, however, where this development has not occurred and where the political parties are strictly non-confessional, as in America, the pre-revolutionary tradition of the Christian state has never been officially disavowed, so that we still preserve the forms of a Christian monarchy and the legal establishment of the Christian Church.

What is the reason for this anomalous state of things which differentiates Europe from both America and Asia? There is no doubt that it is very deeply rooted in the history of the past and it seems to correspond to certain fundamental features of Western cultures. In the first place, I believe that the ideological diversity and tension of modern Europe is comparable to, and to some extent caused by, the religious diversity and tension of post-Reformation Europe. The theological disputes of the Reformation familiarized the masses with ideological issues, and the religious wars of the sixteenth and seventeenth centuries involved the same confusion of convictions, propaganda and power politics with which we are so familiar today. Moreover, the eighteenth century Enlightenment, the source of the modern ideological development, may be regarded historically as a kind of Second Reformation which in certain respects, as, for instance, in the destruction of the temporal power of the Church and the secularization of church property, carried out the work of the earlier Reformation in those parts of Europe which had previously been immune.

Owing to this long familiarity with internal conflict and

controversy, the impact of the new ideologies and the cold war of propaganda between opposing factions has been less devastating in Europe than elsewhere, since European culture can tolerate a much greater degree of internal tension than can other civilizations without losing its sense of continuity and community. This was largely due to the fact that in the past the opposing religions and ideologies of the West possessed a common origin and shared certain common principles and beliefs. Thus, in spite of their intense hostility to one another, Catholics and Protestants all regarded themselves as Christians, and the vast majority on both sides accepted the Bible and the Creeds, and appealed to the teachings of the Fathers in support of their respective principles. Even the theological controversies, which were the source of division, also led to the recognition of common positions and to alliances between different schools of thought, so that Lutherans could support Catholics in their controversy with the Socinians, and Jansenists could support Calvinists in their attack on the Arminians. While religious toleration was practically non-existent and freedom of thought was rare in either camp, a practical modus vivendi was worked out which made it possible for a Catholic like Descartes to live in Holland and Sweden and a Protestant like Leibniz to carry on his correspondence with Bossuet and the French Jesuits on religious problems.

In the same way, the conflicting ideologies of the nineteenth century all shared the common intellectual background of the European Enlightenment. All of them possessed a similar faith in social and scientific progress. All of them were liberal in the sense that they believed in the

Rights of Man and regarded individual liberty, national freedom or social equality as the supreme good. Marx and Mazzini, Blanqui and Bakunin, Proudhon and Louis Blanc were all children of the Revolution and their internecine feuds were like those of the Jacobins and the Girondins in the days of the First Republic.

At the same time, the breach between the ideologies and Christianity was neither complete nor consistent at this period. Between 1830 and 1850 a certain *rapprochement* between them took place, and Liberals like Lamartine, Socialists like Bazard and Democrats like Leroux claimed that their ideas represented a new application of Christian principles to the political and economic spheres. This was especially the case in Great Britain, where the ideologies possessed no revolutionary background. Here Liberalism owed its political influence to its alliance with the Nonconformist Churches, and the Labour movement developed under the leadership of pious Nonconformists and lay preachers like Burt, Fenwick and Keir Hardie. This is not surprising when one remembers that in Great Britain the connection between political opposition and religious dissent dates back to the Puritan revolution of the seventeenth century and that this tradition has never been entirely lost.

This is a tradition which England shares with America, in contrast to the Continent, since the American Revolution, in spite of its close connection with the European Enlightenment, also owed much to the Puritan tradition, which had survived almost intact in New England. In Russia, on the other hand, where the new Western ideologies did not penetrate until the nineteenth century, the opposition between

them and the traditional culture of Orthodox Christendom
was from the beginning conscious and avowed and this is
one of the chief causes that has led to that polar opposition
between Russian Communism and American Democracy
which now divides the world.

Thus it would seem that the political and ideological disunity of Europe in the past has been a source of strength,
as well as of weakness, since in spite of the heavy cost which
this disunity has involved, it has given Europe the opportunity of developing a richer and more many-sided pattern
of life and thought than could have been achieved by a more
unitary type of culture.

Moreover, this tradition of diversity does not date from
the Reformation and the religious divisions of Western
Christendom, although it was accentuated by them. Its origins are much earlier, and it represents something that is
inseparable from the nature of European culture. The origins of Europe as a civilization are due not only to the extension of the higher culture of the old Mediterranean world
to Western and Northern Europe, but also to the dual character of this cultural inheritance. For the culture of the
Later Roman Empire, which was handed on to the Latin
West and the Byzantine East, was compounded of two elements: the classical culture of Greece and Rome and the
religious culture of the Christian Church. Each of these elements possessed its own moral and intellectual traditions,
which were embodied in different literatures, different social
institutions and different ethical systems.

At first glance it seems as though the fall of the Empire
must have involved the disappearance of the classical tradi-

tion, since the Church remained the only link between the barbarian peoples and the civilization of the ancient world; and the monasteries, which were the chief centres of literary culture, were devoted by their institution to the ascetic ideals that seemed most irreconcilable with the spirit of classical humanism. In fact, however, it was the monasteries that secured the survival of the inheritance of classical culture through their adaptation of the old liberal education of the schools of the Later Roman Empire to the needs of the new ecclesiastical culture. This preservation of the old curriculum of the Liberal Arts meant that classical literature remained the basis of Western intellectual training. Virgil and Cicero, Ovid and Seneca, Horace and Quintilian were not merely school books, they became the seeds of a new growth of classical humanism in Western soil. Again and again—in the eighth century as well as in the twelfth and fifteenth centuries—the higher culture of Western Europe was fertilized by renewed contacts with the literary sources of classical culture. At first this influence only reached a small clerical minority, but it steadily increased throughout the later Middle Ages until, by the time of the Renaissance, it became the basis of lay education and inspired the development of vernacular literatures.

In this way the tradition of classical culture, which is also the tradition of humanism, became one of the great formative elements in Western culture. But this did not involve the denial or supersession of the Christian tradition, as has often been suggested by the historians of the Renaissance or the Enlightenment. As the humanist tradition remained alive during the Middle Ages, so the Christian tradition preserved its vitality in the post-Renaissance period, and it is only when both these traditions remain in living and fruitful contact with one another that Western culture attains its highest and most characteristic achievements. Nevertheless, this harmony and sympathetic collaboration between two such diverse traditions is difficult to maintain, and their diversity and tension have manifested themselves throughout the course of European history in those religious and ideological conflicts which I have already discussed. The unity of Europe has always been much more fragile than that of the great civilizations of Asia but at the same time it has been more flexible and more capable than any other culture of assimilating new elements and producing new movements of thought and new forms of social institutions.

Seen from this point of view, the modern ideologies are characteristic products of European culture. They become a symptom of cultural decadence only when they become totalitarian and attempt to destroy the spiritual foundations on which European culture is based. Christianity and humanism are both super-ideological in character. They create ideologies, but are not created by them. Their origins are older than those of Europe itself and they extend their influence far into the unconscious depths of the soul of Western man.

Hence the attempt to confine the whole of Western civilization in the strait-jacket of an ideology and to exclude all cultural and spiritual values which are not created by it or dependent on it is destructive of the inner nature of Western culture and must inevitably lead to disaster.

No doubt the Communist will argue that this is a necessary stage in the evolution of modern culture; that as the feudal Christian order was replaced by the bourgeois humanist order, so the latter must now give place to the new social order of scientific social ideology based on modern science. But if science is divorced from humanism and Christianity, it ceases to be a creative source of culture. It is capable of creating new scientific techniques and technologies but these are the servants of the dominant ideology which, in its turn, is the servant of a political party or dictator. No civilization can live by politics alone, and when a culture becomes merely an organ of political propaganda it is dead.

At the present time the existence of Europe is threatened, first by the ideologies which sprang originally from the revolutionary idealism of the Western mind and its boundless faith in social progress, and secondly by the scientific technologies which were invented to serve the cause of life and which have been perverted to the service of destruction. But this is no longer a purely European problem; it has become a world-wide issue. If the ideological division of the world becomes permanent and complete, and if the new world powers employ all the resources of science and technology in the attempt to destroy one another, it is difficult to see how any civilization can survive anywhere. No doubt Europe would be the first to suffer, but the destruction of Europe would only be the prelude to the destruction of the world.

If, on the other hand, humanity decides not to commit suicide, and the new world powers achieve some kind of modus vivendi or balance of power which makes it possible for them to exist together, as the opposing religious forces in Western Europe managed to coexist after the wars of religion, then Europe will still hold a key position in the development of world culture. For Europe is the only cultural area in which all the ideologies meet, and it is the only culture which still maintains a living contact with the deeper spiritual traditions which underlie and transcend the ideologies.

The creators of the modern ideologies—Marx and Mazzini, John Stuart Mill and Herbert Spencer, Saint-Simon and Comte, Herzen and Proudhon—were all members of the same European society who shared a common background of Western humanist culture, whereas their spiritual descendants and heirs have spread abroad to the four corners of the world, where they are becoming progressively alienated from one another by the influence of the different cultural and racial environments with which they have been identified. Consequently it is in Europe, rather than in Asia or the Antipodes, that the criticism and revision of the ideologies can best be carried out and where they can be made intelligible to one another.

But this is possible only if Western culture retains its vital contact with the two great traditions of Christianity and humanism to which it owes its spiritual existence and its unique world-changing character. The survival of these traditions is far more important than that of European political and economic power, just as the survival of Hellenism was more important than that of the Roman Empire. Consequently, the greatest danger that threatens us is not the external threat to our political independence by the expansion of the new world empires, but the internal disintegration of Western culture by the ideologies which are anti-Christian or anti-humanist.

The fact that these ideologies have become completely identified with political parties, social regimes and military alliances makes them far more impervious to intellectual criticism than they were in their earlier formative phase. On the other hand, the same process which has increased their power has also diminished their spiritual appeal. When the ideologies represented the inner conviction and ideals of a revolutionary intelligentsia or a reformist elite, they aroused a similar psychological response to that of a religious sect. But now that they have become the dogmas of a police state, they have become part of the political organization that they serve.

Now if this situation is clearly recognized in Europe and if Western man agrees to confine the ideologies to their proper sphere and to treat them as alternative programmes of social reform and political action, there is no reason why they should be irreconcilable with the traditions of Western culture. The danger comes from their invasion of the world of religion and metaphysics, so that they claim man's spiritual allegiance even in "the things that are not Caesar's." And they have succeeded in doing so because the spiritual tradition of Western culture had been undermined by that spirit of European nihilism which Nietzsche saw with such tragic intensity in the last century. This nihilism is a peculiarly European disease, a malady of the Western spirit which has extended its influence not only to Russia but also to America. Indeed, nowhere has it found clearer expression than in the writings of a modern American poet like Robinson Jeffers.

This particular development is very closely connected

with the ideologies themselves and is a symptom not, as Nietzsche believed, of the mortal sickness of Christianity and humanism, but rather of the exhaustion of the revolutionary tradition itself. Neither Christianity nor humanism is dead. They still possess an infinite capacity of spiritual regeneration and cultural renaissance. What is passing away is the utopian idealism which was the original inspiration of all the revolutionary ideologies. Now that they have been brought down from the clouds to solid earth they have gained temporal power, but they have lost their old appeal. In so far as they continue to press their total claim to man's spiritual allegiance, they must inevitably drive civilization further and further toward nihilism and self-destruction.

The vital task for Europe at the present time is to resist this tendency and to recover and fortify the two great spiritual traditions which are the roots of its culture. This is a difficult task, and one which cannot be achieved without great moral and intellectual efforts. But it is by no means an impossible task, and since Europe was the original creator of the ideologies, she has a special responsibility and a special opportunity for finding a solution to the problems which the ideologies have raised.

6

Introduction: The Revolt of Asia

THE revolt of Asia is not simply an insurrection against alien domination and the influence of foreign ideas. It is also—and even more—a political and moral revolution in the internal order of the oriental peoples. During the last generation, the oldest and the most fundamental institutions which seemed to be inseparable from Asiatic civilization have lost their sacred prestige and are threatened with change or destruction.

What we are witnessing is, in fact, the extension to Asia and to the whole world of the revolutionary movement of change which started in Western Europe and America in the eighteenth century. As that movement began within the limits of the privileged aristocratic class and was transmitted first to the European *bourgeoisie* and then to the proletariat, so it has spread from the dominant nations of Western Europe—first to Eastern Europe and then to the peoples of Asia and Africa.

Therefore Western man has to shoulder a double responsibility. He is the archetypal revolutionary—the Prometheus who stole fire from heaven and set the world ablaze. Yet at

the same time he is an imperialist, a capitalist and an ex-
ploiter—the obvious target for the criticism and moral in-
dignation of the old peoples of Asia and the new peoples of
Africa whom he has both awakened and enslaved.

This is an awkward and confusing situation for both parties, and we cannot be surprised that the relations between
Europe and Asia should be marked by mutual resentment
and misunderstanding. The men who come to the top in
revolutionary movements are never the wisest or the most
farsighted of men. On the contrary, revolutions provide an
opportunity for the crank, the fanatic and the power maniac,
so that a movement which is inaugurated in a mood of
boundless optimism and generous idealism soon degenerates
into a merciless war of factions and leads through massacre
and persecution to some new form of tyranny.

And a similar process takes place in the sphere of ideology. In the war of ideas, it is the crudest and the most
simplified ideology that wins. During our own lifetimes we
have seen spectacular examples of this. We have seen great
and highly civilized countries becoming infected by epi-
demics of ideological insanity, and whole populations being
destroyed for the sake of some irrational slogan.

In the case of Asia, the situation is fortunately less acute.
The very immensity of the crisis and the fact that the revolution is long drawn out and spread over many different
areas allows us a certain breathing space and an opportunity
to readjust our ideas. At the present time it is difficult to
detach ourselves and view the problem as a whole. For the
politician and the economist are so immersed in the day-to-
day course of the struggle that they cannot look beyond its

immediate effects on their particular society, while the philosopher and the man of letters are apt to be so appalled by the irrationality of the conflicting forces that they avert their eyes to their abstract or private worlds. But for the Christian neither of these alternatives is possible. He is committed not merely by the fact that he shares in the common responsibility of Western men, but because he is obliged to look beyond the political and economic conflicts of the present time to the ultimate spiritual issues on which the fate of the human race depends. For the Christian, no less than the Marxian, has an historical point of view and knows, however obscurely, the goal towards which the world is moving. This view depends on the doctrine of Divine Providence. Whatever else is obscure, it is certain that God is the governor of the universe and behind the apparent disorder and confusion of history there is the creative action of the divine law. Man is a free agent and is continually attempting to shape the world and the course of history to his own designs and interests. But behind the weak power and the blind science of man, there is the overruling purpose of God which uses man and his kingdoms and empires for ends of which he knows nothing and which are often the opposite of those which man desires and seeks to attain.

It may be objected that a theodicy of this kind is of little practical value. If history is carrying man to an unknown goal in obedience to an inscrutable power, there is nothing man can do about it. But the Christian view of history is not just a blind fatalism. It also asserts the principle of divine revelation and admits the possibility of human cooperation with the divine purpose. No doubt man has to

work in the dark, for it is the condition of Christian existence to live by faith and not by sight. Nevertheless, there
are moments when the obscurity of history seems to be suddenly illuminated by some sign of divine purpose. These are
the moments of *crisis* in the literal sense of the word—times
of judgment when the powers of this world are tried and
condemned and when the course of history suddenly flows
into a new channel. Such was the age of the Hebrew prophets, such was the age of St. Augustine, and such is the age
in which we have the privilege and the misfortune to live
today. For the present century has been an apocalyptic age
—a time of judgment in which the established powers and
authorities of the world have been put through the fire and
destroyed or renewed, and when civilizations that have endured for thousands of years are being forced into a new
mould.

The most important factor in this process, both as cause
and result, is the increasing tendency to world unity. It had
its origins centuries ago in the Age of Discovery, when the
Western mariners opened the new oceanic highways and
demonstrated in practice what they had long known in
theory—that the world was round and that there were no
barriers that could not be surmounted by courage and in-
genuity. Thereafter, century by century Western men extended this trade and navigation, until East and West were
drawn closer and closer together by a vast intercontinental
network of trade and communication.

During the present century this process attained its climax. The world was brought even closer together by the
triumphs of Western science and technology. There was a

vast expansion of world population and wealth and a related increase of knowledge and communication.

But these changes have also had a revolutionary effect on politics and culture. In the last fifty years all the historic empires that ruled Asia have fallen, and a multitude of new states and nations have emerged out of the ruins. All these new powers are animated by hostility to Western hegemony and an intense desire to assert their national independence. But at the same time, they are not opposed to the new cosmopolitan civilization which was the fruit of the Western expansion. It is rather that they wish to be active partners in it and to appropriate their full share in the material benefits that it has brought. They are in revolt not merely against the West, but against their own past—against the whole traditional order of the old oriental cultures in which the whole of man's life from the cradle to the grave was bound by custom and precedent, enforced by the sanctions of a sacred law. This twofold revolution is the source of our present problems. The peoples of Asia have been forced against their will into a new cosmopolitan society which is predominantly Western in its principles and values, and at the same time they are reacting violently in defence of their national being. This reaction, however, is not directed against the new world order itself, but against the external powers that gave them a subordinate place in it. This nationalist reaction may easily become reactionary or destructive. In extreme cases, especially in Africa, it may lead to a reaction against civilization itself, and a return to pagan barbarism. But in principle it represents the natural and legitimate protest of societies which have been torn from their old moorings and plunged into a storm of change. Unfortunately the peoples of Asia and Africa have not only to cope with the inherent difficulties of the modern revolution —the sudden change from the pace of the ox to that of the aeroplane; they are being forced to make the change under the aegis of a new form of political organization—the sovereign nation state—which has no roots in their own past. The ancient civilizations of Asia had created their own institutions and social hierarchies, which made it possible for peoples of different languages and religion to follow their own laws and customs without interfering with one another, and this system was often maintained by the Western colonial or imperial powers, notably by the British in India. But the coming of nationalism and the modern nation state has destroyed this traditional modus vivendi and has forced the racial and religious minorities to conform themselves to a common pattern.

Hence the new order in Asia is full of explosive possibilities. Nationalism has nowhere been a force that makes for peace, and the new oriental nationalisms are exceptionally aggressive and intolerant. Nevertheless what they need above all else is peace—internal peace to solve the manifold problems of their new existence, and external peace to avoid a cataclysm which would destroy all the gains of the last half century. The danger of such a catastrophe was never greater than it is today when the Asiatic scene is overshadowed by the cold war between two giant world powers with their rival ideologies and economic systems. But there is still room for the intervention of another factor of a different order. In the past religion has been the greatest of the powers that formed the mind and developed the cultures of the Asiatic peoples. At the present moment it is in eclipse owing to the wave of secular influences that has accompanied the spread of Western culture. But it is too soon to say how far this eclipse will go. Certainly it is not total and there seems little probability that it will ever become so.

This is the most important aspect of the whole oriental problem, and it demands much fuller study than it has yet received. When one considers the amount of study that is being devoted to the purely political aspects of oriental nationalism, Christians cannot but feel ashamed of the little that has been done towards the understanding of the new religious situation arising from the revolutionary changes of the last fifty years. Neither the technological process that is forcing East and West together nor the insurgence of the nationalist forces that is tearing them apart can save the modern world from destruction. Salvation can only come from some power capable of creating a spiritual unity which will transcend and comprehend the material unity of the new world order. And where can this power be found save in religion?

7

Earlier Encounters Between East and West

From time immemorial Asia has been the home of the world empires. Sargon of Akkad, Hammurabi of Babylon, the Kings of the Hittites and the Assyrians, and finally the great Kings of Persia had followed in one another's footsteps over a thousand battlefields until the high road of empire had been beaten flat from the Mediterranean to the Persian Gulf. Europe was a late comer to the field. It was too poor and too warlike to invite conquest, and too weak and unorganized to make a bid for empire, and thus the Greeks were left free to develop their own culture and institutions based on free citizenship and the intense political activity of the independent city states.

But when the Greek professional soldiers and commercial travellers had once become aware of the wealth and weakness of the imperial colossus in Asia, it was only a matter of time before they took a hand in the game of empire. The military genius of Alexander carried the armies of Europe with breathless vehemence from the Nile to the Indus and the Oxus, and the Persian Empire collapsed like a house of cards. Thus began the first age of Western imperialism which lasted for almost a thousand years—from Alexander to Mohammed—first under the Hellenistic kingdoms which were the heirs of Alexander, then under the Romans who took over the Hellenistic inheritance and strengthened it by the armour of Roman authority and law, and finally under the Christian-Roman Emperors of Constantinople who allied themselves with the new world religion which was itself of oriental origin.

Throughout the second half of this whole period the influence of Western imperialism on Asia was balanced by that of oriental culture in Europe, so that Alexandria, Antioch, Rome and Constantinople became the centers of a cosmopolitan civilization. Meanwhile the age of Western predominance had seen the rise of other Asiatic empires. China was united by Shih Huang-ti in 221 B. C. in one of the most formidable despotisms that the world has seen, while India during the same century was united for a time by the empire of Chandragupta Maurya and Asoka.

Finally during the same period, in the empty heart of Asia beyond the Altai Mountains there arose yet another empire, the first of a long series of empires of the Steppes which were destined to exert a far greater influence on world history than their population and their level of culture seemed to warrant. The world of the Steppes was a land ocean which stretched from China to Europe and southwards to Iran and the Pamirs, so that the rise of a new empire in the heart of the Steppes set up a wave of disturbance which did not cease until it had broken against the defences of the civilized empires to the East or West or South. Thus the establishment of the first Hun Empire in the 3rd century B. C. led to the migration of the Yue Chi southwards into Eastern Iran and Northern India. This resulted in the creation of a new Indo-Scythian empire which dominated the highways from India and Persia to China and became the center of an international Buddhist culture.

But the downfall of the Hun empire in the 3rd century A.D. was even more striking in its results, for it was followed by a period of confusion and barbarian invasion, from the consequences of which none of the world empires escaped. The Western section of the Hun confederation moved westward to the Volga and then into the European Steppe, driving before them the Goths and the Alans who in turn broke into the Roman Empire where they finally set up new barbarian kingdoms in Italy and Spain and Southern France. The other main body of the Huns, followed by the allied Turkish people known to the Chinese as the To Pa, invaded Northern and Western China and set up a series of barbarian dynasties which established Buddhism as the state religion of China. Finally, a century later, another wave of barbarians, the "White Huns" or Hepthalites, whose origins are obscure, invaded Persia and India, where their ravages aroused the same horror as those of Attila and the Huns in Europe.

Thus the age of the barbarian invasions in the West was part of a worldwide disaster from which none of the older empires of Asia was exempt. In Europe the setback to civilization was most serious and the process of recovery was slowest. In China, on the other hand, the situation was restored by the end of the 6th century, and in the 7th century, under the early T'ang emperors, Chinese civilization had attained a wider diffusion and a more cosmopolitan character than ever before or since.

But the Chinese were fortunate in that they had only one set of barbarians to contend with. Europe and the Byzantine Empire, on the other hand, had hardly rallied from the barbarian invasion from the Northern Steppes before they had to face a new attack from the barbarians of the deserts of the South.

Moreover these barbarians were also the missionaries of a new religion and their conquests dealt a mortal blow to the Christian civilization of Syria and North Africa. For the expansion of the Arab Empire, in spite of its rapidity, created a religious culture that was extraordinarily enduring, so that, with the single exception of the Spanish peninsula, all the lands that were conquered in the first century of Islam have remained culturally separated from Europe ever since. Thus throughout the early Middle Ages European culture was in a state of decline and the very existence of Western Christendom was in danger, since it was subjected to the convergent pressure of the Moslem powers which controlled Spain and the Western Mediterranean, and the pagan Vikings from Scandinavia who dominated the North Sea and the Atlantic Coast. The Byzantine Empire still preserved the traditions of higher culture in Southeast Europe, but its communications with the West were interrupted or endangered by the intrusion into Central Europe of successive waves of barbarians from the Steppes, such as the Avars and the Magyars, while the seaways were made perilous by Moslem fleets.

The turning point in the fortunes of Europe came with the conversion to Christianity of the Northmen and the Magyars at the beginning of the 11th century—a period when the Islamic world was being transformed by the decline of the Arabic Khalifate and the coming of the Turks.

The latter, who had been for centuries the dominant power in the heart of Asia, like the Huns before them, had gradually infiltrated into Western Asia as allies and mercenary soldiers of the Khalifs in the same way that the Germans had formerly penetrated the Roman Empire as *foederati.* Like the latter, the Turks soon carved out independent states for themselves throughout the Middle East under the nominal authority of the Khalif of Bagdad, who became the puppet of his Turkish guards. In the 11th century these new Turkish kingdoms became the leaders of a new movement of Moslem expansion. In the East they invaded India and gradually destroyed the old centers of Hindu culture from the Indus to the Ganges. In the West they attacked the Byzantine Empire and conquered Asia Minor, which had hitherto been the bulwark of Eastern Christendom.

After the defeat of the Byzantine army at Manzikert in 1071 there was nothing between the Turks and the Aegean. They established their capital at Nicaea (modern Isnik)— only sixty miles from Constantinople—so that the capital itself was in danger.

But at this moment the whole situation was changed by the intervention of the West. The peoples of Western Europe had already shown their strength by the reconquest of Sicily and Spain and the opening of the Western Mediterranean to the trade of the Italian maritime republics. Now in 1095 at the bidding of the Papacy, they launched themselves on the tremendous enterprise of a crusade to succour the Christians of the East against the Turks and to recover the Holy Places from the infidel. The daughter of the Byzantine Emperor has described in unforgettable phrases the impression produced in the capital by the passage of the innumerable hosts that poured into Asia, as though the whole of the West was on the march; and she brings out the mixture of astonishment, disgust and admiration with which the successors of Justinian regarded the reckless lawless chivalry of the West. If these two forces could have cooperated with one another, Eastern Christendom might yet have been saved. The defeat of the Turks by the Crusaders enabled the Byzantine Empire to recover its essential territories in Asia Minor, while Byzantine support enabled the Crusaders to establish their new Christian states in Syria from Antioch and Edessa to Jerusalem.

The emperor Alexius Comnenus (1081-1119) and his successors, John (1119-1143) and Manuel (1143-1180), all showed considerable tact and skill in their dealings with the Franks, and if these relations could have continued for another fifty years the scattered fragments of Eastern Christendom might have been reconstituted in a new international Christian society, for it must be remembered that the population of Asia Minor, Cilicia and Northern Syria and Mesopotamia was still largely Christian. Unfortunately, the last quarter of the 12th century saw a series of misfortunes, misdeeds and mistakes that ruined the Christian cause. In 1176 the plans of the Emperor Manuel were shattered by his disastrous defeat by the Turks at Myrioscephalon, and his death in 1180 was followed by a series of dynastic revolutions and feuds that left the Empire weak and divided. In 1187 the defeat of the Frankish knights at Hattin in Galilee was followed by the fall of the Kingdom of Jerusalem.

But these misfortunes, instead of uniting the Christians, only served to increase their divisions. The favor which the great emperors of the 12th century had shown towards the Latins was profoundly unpopular with the clergy and people of Constantinople and during the minority of Manuel's son, Alexius II, they rose against the regency of the French-born Empress, Mary of Antioch, and carried out a wholesale massacre of the Latin population of Constantinople in which the papal legate was murdered and all the Latin churches destroyed. From this time onwards, a bitter feud divided the two Christian peoples and their churches. The Franks treated the "Griffons" as an inferior and alien race, while the Greeks regarded the Latins with more bitter enmity then they felt towards the Turks. Already during the Third Crusade in 1189-1190 the German Emperor Frederick I and his son Henry VI contemplated the capture of Constantinople, while the Byzantine emperor on his side entered into relations with Saladin.

Thus the stage was set for the tragedy of the Fourth Crusade. The French crusaders were easily persuaded by the Venetians to turn aside in order to restore the son of the deposed emperor, Alexius IV, who was friendly to the West, and when the restored emperor was deposed and murdered in a popular uprising, it was only too easy to abandon all attempts for a settlement, to sack the city, to overthrow the government and to establish a new Latin empire of Constantinople, after the pattern of the crusading states of Antioch and Jerusalem.

But the Latin empire marked the bankruptcy of the crusading idea. Instead of the restoration of Eastern Christendom, it meant the exploitation of its weakness by groups of French adventurers and Italian merchant princes. The Byzantine empire survived in Asia Minor, but its energies were now devoted not to the defence of Christendom against Islam, but to the reconquest of its European provinces from the West.

But while Eastern Christendom was undergoing this process of disintegration, Islam was itself threatened from a totally unexpected quarter. At the beginning of the 13th century a Mongol chieftain, Temuchin, afterwards known as Chingis Khan, welded the nomad peoples beyond the Altai into a new empire of the Steppes and forthwith started on a career of world conquest. In the course of thirty years the Mongol armies swept across Asia and East Europe, destroying anything that stood in their path from the Yellow Sea to the Adriatic and from North Russia to Northern India. Finally in 1257 they attacked Mesopotamia and destroyed the Khalifate of Bagdad. Thus a new world empire was created, with its center at Karakorum, south of Lake Baikal, which included China and Turkestan and Persia and Russia.

Islam was the greatest sufferer from this revolution, since it meant that the great centers of Moslem culture in Persia and Mesopotamia were devastated and subjected to the yoke of a pagan and barbarous people.

But for Western Europe it was far from being an unmixed disaster. It relieved the Christians from the pressure of Islam which had lain so heavily upon them for five hundred years. The Mongols, in spite of their ruthlessness, were by no means intolerant. Their rulers intermarried freely with Nestorian Christian wives, and they welcomed Western merchants and artificers at their courts.

Thus for the first time in history Europe became aware of the wider Asiatic world beyond the frontiers of Islam. The Christian kingdom of Prester John might be a mirage, but Cathay and India were solid realities, and by the end of the 13th century there was a Franciscan archbishop at Peking and Italian merchants at the Chinese ports. Even more remarkably, a Tartar bishop from Peking was sent on an embassy to Europe from the Mongols in 1287 and celebrated the East Syrian liturgy in the presence of the Pope and Cardinals. But the *pax Mongolian* which opened the road from Europe to China did not last long, and when the Mongol empire fell in 1368 the door between East and West was closed more completely than ever. The Chinese nationalists destroyed the foreign colonies, while the revival of Islam in Central Asia finally liquidated the last remains of Nestorian Christianity in Central Asia, as well as the scattered Western missionaries in Turkestan and India.

The empire of the Steppes was indeed reconstituted for the last time in history by Timur (1336-1406), a Barlas Turk from Transoxiana, a more sinister and destructive figure than any of his Mongol predecessors. The latter had at least created a kind of peace and an enduring world empire, however great the cost in human misery. But Timur seems to have been animated by a disinterested love of destruction for its own sake, and he left nothing behind but the pyramids of skulls which marked his path from the Ganges to the Volga and the Aegean.

In the course of these homicidal wanderings he destroyed the headquarters of the Western merchants at Taiva at the mouth of the Don and the great market of Sarai on the Volga, thus closing the great Mongol trade route which had linked Europe with Central Asia and China. It is true that his foray into Asia Minor gave a breathing space for the Byzantine Empire in its last struggle with the Ottoman Turks, who had been steadily advancing into Southeast Europe since the middle of the 14th century, but it had no effect on the ultimate results, which detached the whole of the Balkan peninsula from Europe for four centuries and finally put an end to European economic and cultural expansion in the Levant.

Nevertheless throughout this period Western Christendom, in spite of its political disunity, was full of life and energy, and the commercial activity of the Italian cities was greater than ever before. Thus the closing of the Eastern Mediterranean by the advance of the Turkish power led the Western peoples to look for a new solution by turning the flank of Islam and finding a new way of access to the markets of Asia by way of the Western ocean. This was finally achieved by the Genoese and Portuguese navigators, whose efforts were first turned in this direction by Prince Henry of Portugal (1394-1460), afterwards known as the Navigator.

8

The Age of Discovery[1]

THE change in the world position of Europe which has taken place during the last fifty years has inevitably caused a strong reaction against the spirit of nineteenth-century imperialism. The idea of empire has become identified with the oppression of subject peoples, and the whole colonial development is regarded as a form of economic exploitation. Yet the imperialist phase of Western culture is not confined to the second half of the nineteenth century. It was the culmination of a much wider movement which goes back to the close of the Middle Ages and which has been one of the main forces in the formation of the modern world. However great may be our moral disapproval of *Homo Europaeus* in his relations with weaker and more primitive peoples, we cannot ignore his positive achievements, for they have changed the face of the earth and created a new world, or even a number of new worlds. Consequently it is impossible to understand the nature of the present world crisis apart from the Western movement of colonial expansion which has transformed the closed Mediterranean continental world

[1] This chapter contains brief excerpts from *Understanding Europe* (New York, 1952), *Religion and the Rise of Western Culture* (New York, 1950), and *The Judgment of the Nations* (New York, 1942).

of ancient and medieval culture into an oceanic civilization which has unified the world.

As I wrote concerning the nature of that process ten years ago: "How did it come about that a small group of peoples in Western Europe should in a relatively short space of time acquire the power to transform the world and to emancipate themselves from man's age-long dependence on the forces of nature? In the past this miraculous achievement was explained as the manifestation of a universal Law of Progress which governed the universe and led mankind by inevitable stages from apehood to perfection. Today such theories are no longer acceptable, since we have come to see how much they depend on an irrational optimism which was part of the phenomenon they attempted to explain. Instead we now tend to ask ourselves what were the factors in European culture which explain the peculiar achievement of Western man? or to use the brutal and expressive American phrase, 'What makes him tick?' But when we reach this point we shall find the religious factor does have a very important bearing upon the question.

"For, side by side with the natural aggressiveness and the lust for power which are so evident in European history, there were also new spiritual forces driving Western man towards a new destiny. The activity of the Western mind, which manifested itself alike in scientific and technical invention as well as in geographical discovery, was not the natural inheritance of a particular biological type; it was the result of a long process of education which gradually changed the orientation of human thought and enlarged the possibilities of social action.

"The other great world cultures realized their own syn-

thesis between religion and life and then maintained their
sacred order unchanged for centuries and millennia. But
Western civilization has been the great ferment of change
in the world, because the changing of the world became an
integral part of its cultural ideal."[2]

There is no doubt, however, that the rapid material progress and external expansion of Western culture has coincided with its increasing secularization, so that the religious
element seems less prominent in the very period when the
influence of Western civilization has been most widespread,
and this in turn has meant the spread of a secularized culture throughout the world. Now it is true that world empires usually tend to lose touch with their spiritual roots,
and the same factor may be seen at work in the expansion
of a civilization by way of administrative and intellectual
influence, as in the Hellenistic world culture in the third and
second centuries B.C. However, this is not the basic cause
for the process of secularization which has occurred. For
Western culture was becoming secularized before the great
period of its expansion had begun. The fundamental causes
of that process were spiritual and closely related to the
whole spiritual development of Western Man. But the same
causes which produced the secularization of culture were
also responsible for its external expansion. They were, in
fact, two aspects of a single process, a world revolution of
such a tremendous kind that it seems to transcend history
and create new categories with which our traditional standards of judgment are incapable of dealing.

It is with regard to the religious issue that the traditional

2 *Religion and the Rise of Western Culture*, pp. 8, 10.

methods of interpretation are most defective. For if we consider the problem from a Christian point of view we are faced by the paradox that it was a Christian culture and not a pagan one which was the source of this revolution. While the secular historian is brought up against the equally disturbing fact that the non-secular element in Western culture has been the dynamic element in the whole process of change, so that the complete secularization of culture by removing this element would bring the progressive movement to a full stop, and thus bring about a static society which has mastered social change to such a degree that it no longer possesses any vital momentum.

Nevertheless the new lay humanist culture which was beginning to develop in the West in the fifteenth and sixteenth centuries was far from being entirely secular. As Burdach has shown, the very conception of the Renaissance—or the rebirth of culture—was closely connected with the Reformation or the rebirth of Christianity. Both were influenced in their origins by the apocalyptic hopes of a spiritual renewal of Christendom, which was so widespread in the later Middle Ages and which found different forms of expression in Northern and Southern Europe. Neither the Humanists nor the Reformers dreamt of the destruction of Christendom. They believed, like Erasmus, that "the world was coming to its senses as if awakening out of a deep sleep," and they thought that religion and culture could slough off their old skins and could renew their youth by returning to their origins.

Thus the Renaissance achievement was like that of Columbus, who discovered the new world by attempting to

find his way back to the old world by a new route. The
sudden removal of the fixed limits which had bounded the
thought and action of medieval man, the opening of new
worlds and the realization of the boundless possibilities of
human reason caused a release of energies which gave Western culture a new world-embracing character. Though Western science was still in its infancy, men like Leonardo da
Vinci and Paracelsus and Campanella and Bacon had already begun to realize its world-transforming possibilities:

> Glory to Him who knows and can do all [writes Campa-
> nella]:
> O my art, grandchild to the Primal Wisdom, give some-
> thing of his fair image which is called Man.
> A second God, the First's own miracle, he commands the
> depths; he mounts to Heaven without wings and counts its
> motions and measures and its natures.
> The wind and the sea he has mastered and the earthly
> globe with pooped ship he encircles, conquers and beholds,
> barters and makes his prey.
> He sets laws like a God. In his craft, he has given to silent
> parchment and to paper the power of speech and to distin-
> guish time he gives tongue to brass.

The author of these verses is a striking example of the way
in which the thought of the Renaissance united humanist
and scientific culture with apocalyptic religious ideals and
revolutionary hopes for a new order of society.

Despite the frustration of the idealistic hopes of the Renaissance for the creation of a new social order, in one respect
the age of the Renaissance gave birth to a practical result
of incalculable importance, which altered the whole future

of the world. This was the great movement of navigation and discovery, which at last broke the bounds of the old Mediterranean world and opened the new ocean routes to America and the East. And although these discoveries had a disastrous effect on the commercial prosperity of Italy, it was Italian enterprise above all that rendered them possible. The trading states of Italy were the schools of medieval navigation. They developed the new types of ocean-going ships, and introduced from the Moslem East, as early as the twelfth century, the magnet, as well as the use of the astrolabe and the timepiece without which scientific navigation was impossible. Moreover, it was the Venetians, Marco Polo and his uncles, who first reached China and circumnavigated Asia from Zeitun to the Persian Gulf in the latter part of the thirteenth century and fired the imagination of Europe with their tales of the boundless wealth and population of the East.

The initiation of the great period of discovery was due above all, however, to the vision and tenacity of one man, the Portuguese Prince Henry, afterwards known as the Navigator, who, for more than forty years, from his palace observatory of Sagres on the "Sacred Cape" of Saint Vincent sent out expedition after expedition down the West African coast. He was not a man of the Renaissance, but a pious and ascetic prince after the medieval fashion, who aimed, above all, at gaining a new world for Christendom to compensate for what had been lost to the infidel in the Levant. But he made full use of Italian science and Italian enterprise, and some of his most able captains, like the Venetian Cadamosto, were of Italian origin. And so too in later years it was Italians like the Cabots, and Amerigo Vespucci, Verrazano and, above all, Columbus himself, who were the great pioneers of exploration in the service of the Western powers. The discovery of America by Columbus, and of the Cape route to India by the Portuguese had an immediate and profound effect upon European history. Not only did it revolutionize the trade routes of the old world, it destroyed the age-long eastbound orientation of European culture. The effect on Renaissance Italy was especially important. For three centuries Italy had dominated the Eastern Mediterranean. The prosperity of Genoa was derived from the trade with the Black Sea and that of Venice from that with India by way of Egypt. For a thousand years Italy had been in contact with the Byzantine culture, and in the fifteenth century this influence was stronger than ever owing to the presence of Byzantine scholars like Bessarion and George of Trebizond.

Now, almost simultaneously, her control of the Aegean was threatened by the Turkish conquest, and her monopoly of the oriental trade was destroyed by the new discoveries. The Atlantic ports of Lisbon and Cadiz and Antwerp took the place of Venice and Genoa as the great marts of foreign wares. The Mediterranean, which had been the highway of trade and culture since prehistoric times, suddenly became a backwater.

At the same time, with the conquest of Egypt in 1517 and of Hungary from 1520 to 1530, the whole of the Eastern world from the Danube to the Red Sea was united under the Turkish power, which was far more hostile and dangerous to European culture than the Sultanate of Egypt had ever been.

These changes affected the trade of Venice with extraordinary swiftness. By the year 1509 the Egyptian trade had declined to vanishing point. Nevertheless she held the fragments of her Aegean empire, Cyprus until 1571, Crete until 1669, and preserved some prosperity, as did the rest of North Italy, by industry and trade with Northern Europe. But to these economic catastrophes was added the disaster of foreign invasions and the French and Spanish conquests, which finally put an end to the great age of Italian civilization.

The change of conditions was slower in affecting the Southern German trading cities. In fact, at the beginning of the sixteenth century, their prosperity was at its height and the great capitalist houses of the Fugger and the Welser occupied the same position of international importance that the Florentine bankers had held a century earlier. The towns of Southern Germany, above all Nuremberg and Augsburg, and those of the Rhineland were the scene of a short-lived German Renaissance. It was here that the new arts of printing and engraving were developed—scientists like Peuerbach and Regiomontanus, artists like Dürer and Cranach, scholars like Erasmus of Rotterdam and Reuchlin, rivalled their Italian contemporaries. Nevertheless, the centre of gravity had been moved Westward, and it was the Atlantic powers, Spain, France, England and the Netherlands, that were to dominate the following age, both economically and politically.

The motives which inspired this movement of exploration and discovery which shifted the axis of world power from the Mediterranean to the Atlantic were mixed in character. First there was the religious motive, the continuance of the medieval crusading ideal, which is especially clear in the work of Prince Henry, the great precursor of the Age of Discovery, who conceived the idea of turning the flank of the Moslem world power by the exploration of West Africa and the establishment of a new Christian dominion in Guinea. Nor was it an accident that the discovery of America by Spain was the immediate sequel to the capture of Granada, which ended the long history of the Spanish Reconquest. But from the first the commercial motive also played a great part, especially in the Italian maritime states which had suffered most from the closing of the old trade routes to the East. Yet this economic motive had also existed in the early crusading movement, so far as the participation of the Italian states was concerned. But in the case of Spain, and to a lesser degree of Portugal and France, an attempt was made to subordinate the purely economic factor to the old crusading ideal. The Spanish conquest of America and the French settlement of Quebec and Montreal were thoroughly medieval in spirit. It was the aim of the Spanish government to create a new Christendom across the seas, and the search for gold and land was accompanied by a no less genuine missionary enthusiasm. This motive led the Crown to interpose between the greed of the colonists and the native populations. It inspired the career of Las Casas and the enlightened Indian legislation of the Spanish government, which, however imperfectly carried out, at least saved the native population from extinction. Its most remarkable expression, however, was in the mission states, notably that of the Jesuits in Paraguay, and later that of the Franciscans in California, which forms a unique chapter in colonial history.

The spirit of the Dutch colonial enterprise, on the other hand, is completely different. To them above all is due the creation of a purely economic colonial policy. They came as traders, not as conquerors, still less as missionaries, and their possessions were administered entirely with a view to the interests of the shareholders in the great colonial joint-stock companies, such as the East India Company. The Dutch were the great pioneers of the new colonial and commercial system; and the English, and, from the time of Colbert, the French also, followed in their footsteps. But while the English adopted the Dutch system of commercial colonization and colonial companies, they differed from the Dutch in the predominantly agricultural character of their American colonies; and the consequent growth of a large homogeneous agricultural population across the Atlantic was to have a vast importance for the future development of civilization in the new world.

In addition to the religious and economic factors behind the movement of exploration and colonization, one cannot exclude the influence of two other motives—scientific curiosity and the love of travel, navigation and adventure for their own sakes. Now all these four motives also operated in the case of the Islamic expansion, and the West was thus following in the steps of the earlier oriental movement. To some extent the two movements were contemporaneous, since the Portuguese and Dutch colonization of the East Indies took place at the same period that Mohammedan traders and missionaries were advancing in Indonesia and conquering the older Hindu cultures that had dominated the regime.

For all that, the European expansion had a new and revo-

lutionary character that distinguished it from all that had
gone before. In the course of a single generation—between
1486 and 1536—the world was suddenly transformed by a
series of voyages and discoveries—the circumnavigation of
Africa, the discovery of America, the discovery of India and
the Far East for Western trade, the circumnavigation of the
world, and the conquest of Mexico and Peru. All this represents an extraordinary explosion of human energy, for
none of their results were achieved without hazards of navigation and disease—above all scurvy. (Of Magellan's five
ships only one returned, and of the 270 or 280 men only
35; nor was this an exceptionally bad record.)

In the case of Portugal, it is at first sight difficult to explain how these small expeditions of small ships from one
of the smallest of European states should have been able to
establish a colonial empire throughout the East, from East
Africa to Malaya and Indonesia, in the face of organized
opposition from Egypt and the commercial states of Western India and Indonesia. For these powers possessed all the
advantages of fighting on their own ground, close to their
own bases and supported by the religious sympathies of the
local populations. The phenomenon is undoubtedly a complex one which involves many factors of diverse origin and
value. But beyond all the temporary and accidental factors
the Age of Discovery also seems to represent the energies
of a new type of man and a new attitude to the world which
was to remain characteristic of this new phase of Western
culture. This new type was the product of the impact of
humanism on Christian culture and their combined influence
on the material expansion of the Western European nations,
whose superabundant energies, like those of the Turks and

Mongols, may perhaps be explained biologically as a result of the pressure of population on territory and food supply. (And this last factor may explain why the smallest countries, like Portugal, England and the Netherlands, played such a leading part in the development.) In the Middle Ages, both in the East and the West, there was no lack of interest in travel and exploration and economic enterprise, as we see from the records of the Moslem and Christian travellers like Ibn Batuta and Marco Polo, but there was at the same time a certain moral disapproval and feeling that there was something impious in exceeding the bounds that had been set out by God and Nature on human achievement. We find a popular expression of this in the *Arabian Nights,* where Sindbad, who is inspired by a spirit of enterprise and adventure like an Elizabethan's, feels compelled to apologize for his adventurousness as morally wrong—"My wicked soul suggested to me to travel again to the countries of other people and I felt a longing for associating with the different races of men and for selling and gains."

Even more remarkable is Dante's passage on the last voyage of Ulysses, which seems to express prophetically the new ideal that was to inspire Western man. "O brothers who through a hundred thousand perils have reached the West, do not grudge to the brief space of consciousness that remains to gain experience beyond the sun of the uninhabited world. Consider your origin. You were not made to live like animals, but to seek virtue and knowledge." Yet Dante does not approve of this heroism. He speaks of it as "a mad voyage" and suggests that the fate of the explorers was a just retribution for their folly.

With the Renaissance, the public opinion changed and

the humanists from Politian onwards regard the discoveries in the spirit of Dante's Ulysses. Yet the great poet of the movement, Camoëns, who himself spent most of his life in India and the Moluccas and China in the course of Western expansion and who represents better than any other writer the union of the crusading spirit and the humanist ideal, also gives expression to the traditional medieval feeling in the long speech of the old man of Lisbon at the end of Canto 4, protesting against the false ideals that inspired the colonial movement. "This folly which describes as enterprise and valour what is but the cruel ferocity of the brute creation and boasts of its contempt of life which should always be held dear."[2]

In fact one of the remarkable features of the new European movement is the way in which it has always been accompanied by a spirit of criticism and self-questioning—indeed it is one of the sources of the self-questioning of Western man. Thus the conquest of America led to the Christian humanitarian propaganda of Las Casas—the first of the long series of protests against colonial and imperialist exploitation and of the defence of the rights of native peoples; and in the same way the oriental expansion was accompanied by a tendency towards the appreciation of the value of the oriental cultures. This dualism is the inevitable result of the internal contradictions of European expansion—on the one hand, the economic desire for trade and gold and the exploitation of the new lands, and on the other the missionary call to spread the faith and the Kingdom of God.

[2] From W. C. Atkinson's translation of the *Luciads*, p. 120. (Penguin Classics.)

As I have said, both these motives were already present in the crusading movement, and one recalls the utterances of Franciscan reformers like Roger Bacon and Ramon Lull, who complain that the spiritual purposes of the crusade were stultified by the greed and oppression of the representatives of Christendom. But after the Age of Discovery the contradiction was more glaring, and by the seventeenth century the two aspects of the movement become increasingly divergent and express themselves through different channels.

One, the economic movement, finds its appropriate organ in the great trading companies, above all the Dutch East India Company, which embodied the economic motive in its most marked and ruthless form, especially under the leadership of the great organizer and builder of Dutch rule in Indonesia, Jan Pieterzoon Coen (1586–1627). In the same way the missionary movement was embodied in the religious orders, especially the Jesuits, whose members were often drawn from peoples like the Italians who were not politically involved in the movement of colonial expansion and who did their best to assimilate themselves to their non-European environment. Nevertheless the dominant tendency throughout this whole period was to maintain a close bond between economic, political and religious expansion. This was the policy of Spain in America and the Philippines, of Portugal in Africa and Asia, and of France in Canada, and it was responsible for the destruction of the great work of the Portuguese mission in Japan and Indonesia and ultimately for the decline of the Jesuit mission in China.

It must be emphasized that throughout this period the West had made no impression on the power centres of the oriental world. The great Asiatic empires—Turkey, Persia, the Mogul Empire of Hindustan and China—remained intact; even Japan and Abyssinia were strong enough to exclude Western influence, though this was represented as yet only by missionaries who did not attempt political domination. On the other hand, the West had obtained almost complete mastery of the seas and of maritime trade, and it had conquered the New World of America which was to take an increasingly important part in the balance of world power. This Empire of the Seas was accompanied by an immense growth of scientific knowledge and a technological advance in shipbuilding, navigation and cartography, which laid the foundations of the European world hegemony of the following age.

9

The Fall of the Oriental Empires

DURING the eighteenth and nineteenth centuries, the influence of Western culture began to penetrate the inner continental areas of Asia and Africa, and the historic oriental empires underwent a rapid decline. The first step in this process was the Europeanization of Russia, which had remained for centuries a kind of intermediate zone between Europe and Asia. In the seventeenth century Russian power had expanded rapidly across northern Asia, reaching Okhotsk on the Pacific before the middle of the century, but Russia itself remained outside the sphere of Western culture. It was the revolutionary work of Peter the Great from 1689 to 1725 that forced Russia against its will to become part of Europe. The process was primarily military, secondly technological and industrial, thirdly educational and scientific and fourthly social and artistic. None of these aspects was neglected by Peter, but it was his insistence on the importance of technological change that distinguishes him from his contemporaries and most of his successors. On the other hand the violence and oppressiveness with which he enforced his reforms caused a permanent trauma in mod-

ern Russian culture which shows itself in the Russian revolutionary movement. This was the work of the Europeanized
intelligentsia, but it was at the same time a revolt against
Petrine Russia.

While the new Russia was extending a modified form of
Western culture into the heart of Asia, the old colonial powers were increasing their commercial and maritime pressure,
and the decay of the Mogul Empire in continental India created a political vacuum which was filled by the economic
power of the East India Company out of which arose the
British Empire in India. Now for the first time the higher
culture of the East came under direct Western influence,
and though the process of penetration was a very gradual
one, it was a continuous one which eventually transformed
the traditional order of Indian culture. British rule in India
differed in important respects from all the other imperial
and colonial Empires in history—not only from the Roman
and the Spanish Empires, but also from Dutch and French
colonial movements. This was due to the fact that it was an
authoritarian system based on laissez-faire principles. It was
the policy of the East India Company to insert itself into
the political structure of post-Mogul India with as little disturbance as possible of existing social and economic relations. As Wellington once wrote: "The principle of our
occupation of India has been the protection of the property
in land in the hands of the natives; and with a view to the
attainment of this object the positive prohibition of colonization by Europeans and of the purchase of land by Europeans out of the boundaries of the original settlements."
Thus India was a sort of vast native reserve administered by

the Company as the representative of the Mogul empire, to maintain law and order for the benefit of the native population and of course of the Company itself, which held the monopoly of the trade between India and Europe on the one hand, and India and China on the other. On these principles the Company was not concerned with the spread of Western civilization in India. Its rule was *quieta non moveri,* and it looked askance at the activities of Christian missionaries, and any attempt by social reformers to interfere with Indian customs. It assimilated itself to its surroundings, using Persian as its official language and administering the law according to Islamic and Brahmin codes. Change was inevitable, but it did not come from the government but from the force of circumstances.

Thus the Protestant missionaries based themselves on the Danish settlements of Serampore in Bengal and Tranquebar in the South, but though they had entered India by the back door without the Company's permission, it was difficult for the governors, who were themselves Christians, to deport or silence them. In the same way it was impossible to create an efficient administrative and legal system without introducing reforms that were based consciously or unconsciously on Western ideas. Above all some form of higher education for the Company's employees was indispensable, and as early as the time of Warren Hastings this led to the first real cultural contacts between India and Europe. Hastings was himself a student of oriental literature, and sponsored the first translation of the Bhagavad-Gita in 1785. In 1784 the Asiatic Society of Bengal was founded, and in 1792 the Sanskrit College at Benares. But it was the foundation of the

College at Fort William by Lord Wellesley in 1800 that was
epoch-making, since it led to the first use of the vernacular
languages in education, and this involved the writing of text-
books and the creation of a prose literature in Urdu and
Hindi. Thus the origins of the new prose literature not only
in Urdu and Hindi, but also in Bengali and the other ver-
naculars arose out of the demands of the new educational
system, which was itself a product of the contact of European and Indian culture. A large share in this work was
taken by the Protestant missionaries from Serampore, especially Carey and Marshman who became teachers at Fort
William College, though that institution remained strictly
non-Christian. And missionaries took a similar part in the
teaching and printing of the Dravidian vernacular languages
of Southern India.

In the course of time, however, there was an increasing
demand and need for the study of English, and from the
time of Macaulay's famous *Minute on Education* in 1835,
it became the policy of the Government to provide a stand-
ardized type of secular, higher education in the English
language throughout the country, and it was this common
education which in the course of a century became the basis
of modern Indian nationality. This is fully recognized by the
Indian nationalists themselves, such as Sardar Panikkar,
who writes as follows: "In the first place the system of higher
education in English provided India with a class imbued
with social purposes foreign to Hindu thought. The continuity and persistence of those purposes achieved the socio-
religious revolution on which the life of modern India is
based. While British administration did little or nothing to

emancipate the spirit, to extinguish the prejudices, to eradi-
cate the ravages of ignorant custom and pernicious superstition, the New Learning which came to India through its
introduction to the English language on a nation-wide scale
undoubtedly did all this. Indeed it may be argued that the
essential contradiction of the British rule in India lay in this:
the constituted government upheld the validity of customs,
maintained and administered laws which denied the principles of social justice, refused to legislate for changes ur-
gently called for by society, watched with suspicion the
movement of liberal ideas, while the officially sponsored and
subsidized educational system was undermining everything
that the Government sought to uphold. . . . In the educational system the Government created and maintained an
opposition to itself in a place where its own methods were
ineffectual.

"The mining of the ancient fortress of Hindu custom was
a major achievement, for the reason that it was uniformly
spread all over India. Had the new education been through
the vernacular languages, the emphasis of the movement
would have been different from province to province. . . .
There would have been no 'master plan' of change, and instead of the Hindu community being unified, it would have
split into as many units as there are languages in India. . . .
From this development India was saved by the common
medium of education which Macaulay introduced into India.

"In the second place it is a point of major significance in
the evolution of India as a single nation that this uniform
system of education throughout India through a single language produced a like-mindedness on which it was possible

to build. That it gave to India a common language for political thinking and action is of less importance than the
creation of this like-mindedness, this community of thought,
feeling and ideas which created the Indian nationality."[1]

Thus it is clear that the success of the British policy in
India was due to this combination of political conserva-
tism and educational liberalism. If the Government had attempted to carry out a drastic programme of social reform
to modernize Indian culture, it would have united the whole
population in a vehement resistance to Western influences:
if on the other hand it had followed the advice of the orientalists on the educational commission and had supported a
purely traditional type of education based on Sanskrit and
Persian and Brahui, Indian culture would have remained
isolated and unchanged. The result of the dualist policy was
to create a native Indian demand for social and political
reform which has led (as Sardar Panikkar shows) to the
transformation of the traditional Hindu society into something new. But he does not make it sufficiently clear that
this result was foreseen and planned by the founders of the
system. In his *Minute on Education,* Macaulay compares
the situation in India to that in Russia a hundred years earlier, and it is clear that he envisaged not merely a limited
educational reform, but a far-reaching process of cultural
transformation through the influence of education.

The first fruits of this process were already visible before
Macaulay wrote in the work of Ram Mohun Roy, the great
Bengali leader who initiated the liberal reform of Indian cul-

[1] *Asia and Western Dominance* by K. M. Panikkar. Reprinted by permission of The John Day Company, publisher.

ture. Thus it preceded the introduction of Western technology, which was slow to come in India and began only with the construction of the Indian railways and telegraph under Lord Dalhousie, 1848–56. On the other hand the missionaries (mainly the Protestant missionaries) played a great part in the movement from the beginning. Not only did they provide teachers and linguists for the new educational system (as at Fort William College), but they were the only people who attempted to provide primary education, and through their schools they produced a far deeper impression than they did by their preaching. Yet their religious propaganda also had an important effect in awakening the Indian mind and producing the criticism and restatement of Hindu doctrine which were expressed in the new reformist movements of the Brahmo Samaj of Ram Mohun Roy and the Arya Samaj of Dayananda Sarasvati.

Now the same process that proved so effective in India also affected China in the following period. Here as in India, the coming of Western influence was primarily the work of the European trader—in fact of the same traders' organization—the East India Company, whose trade was based on the exchange of the two staples—tea and opium. But here the resistance of the Asiatic polity to European infiltration and to Western culture was far stronger and more effective. The mere establishment of diplomatic relations involved two wars. For Chinese culture was such a highly integrated system, so politically centralized and so socially uniform, that it was difficult for Western culture to penetrate it without destroying it. On the other hand the Chinese empire was undergoing a rapid process of decay all through the nineteenth century, just as the Mogul empire in India had done in the eighteenth century. The great Ch'ing emperors of the seventeenth and eighteenth centuries had raised Chinese prestige and also Chinese self-sufficiency to a point which their successors were unable to maintain. The eunuch-ridden court and the tradition-ridden bureaucracy were incapable alike of resisting the pressure of Western commerce and of controlling popular discontent, which exploded in the great popular rising of the T'ai P'ing rebels, who found their inspiration in the new doctrines preached by Western missionaries. If the Western powers had supported the rebels, the Ch'ing dynasty would have come to an end fifty years earlier than it did, and would have been replaced by a native Christian or semi-Christian new order instead of by a Communist one. Instead, the English and the Americans used their influence to support the government in return for the opening of the country to Western traders and missionaries. Gordon helped to suppress the T'ai P'ing, and later Robert Hart reorganized the Chinese customs service with considerable benefit to the national finances. In this, both Gordon and Hart acted as servants of the Chinese empire and formed a temporary buffer between the old system and the pressure of Western powers. At the same time, the missionaries, under the protection of the Western treaties, increased this propaganda and attempted to establish schools and hospitals. It was largely through their influence that during the second half of the nineteenth century some attempt was made by Chinese reformers, like Yung Wing, to acquire Western knowledge and to send students to America and Europe. But these attempts were frustrated by the dead hand of official traditionalism, and by the sinister influence of the Empress and the court eunuchs. It was not until the Japanese war of 1894 that China was forced to face the need for modernization. Even then the party of reform, though supported by the Emperor, was defeated by the Dowager Empress, who for her part supported the anti-foreign reaction of the Boxer Movement. This was the most disastrous mistake ever committed by a responsible government, since it led to the complete defeat and discredit of the Empire, and rendered the Chinese revolution of the twentieth century inevitable.

The history of the penetration of Western culture into Japan offers an extraordinary contrast to the case of China. Japan had excluded Western influence—and especially missionary influence—far more drastically than China for more than 200 years. Yet the acceptance of Western culture in the second half of the nineteenth century was extraordinarily rapid and successful, and it resulted in Japan achieving an international status as a world power which distinguished it from all other non-Western states. What is the explanation of this remarkable achievement?

In the first place Japan was the only country of Asia which accepted the necessity of Westernization with open eyes, and deliberately set herself to control the process of modernization in the interests of the nation as a whole. In the second place, the reform coincided with an internal political revolution which was not due to Western influence, but had the authority and prestige of the sacred monarchy behind it. And thirdly the reforms were carried out by an exceptionally able· group of statesmen—Prince Ito, Okubo

Toshimichi, Kido Junichiro, and Goto Shojiro—such as were not to be found in any other Asiatic country at the time. The credit for this must be ascribed in some measure to the old system that they replaced, for the Tokuyawa regime had instilled into the ruling (Samurai) classes an exceptionally high standard of social discipline and responsibility. Indeed the moral ideal of the Legacy of Ieyasu expresses a spirit of stern self-repression and moral activism which has much in common with the Western traditions of Stoicism and Puritanism. It was this spirit of social discipline which enabled the reformers to overcome the xenophobia of the conservative opposition, which was as violent as anything to be found in China or in Islam. In 1858 their leader, Mito Nariaki, one of the most influential men in Japan, went so far as to demand that the negotiators of the Treaty with America should be forced to commit suicide and that the American minister himself should be decapitated. For a time anyone who carried an umbrella was liable to be cut down by swordsmen who resented this badge of foreign barbarism! Nevertheless in a few years the whole people was induced to abandon the cherished laws and customs of the past, to adopt European dress, European laws and a European constitution.

But these sacrifices were not unrewarded. Population and wealth increased, and above all, the naval and military power of Japan advanced with startling rapidity. The war with China in 1894–5 made her the strongest power in Asia, and the Russo-Japanese war in 1904–5 showed that she could meet and defeat one of the greatest military powers of the West. This war marks a turning point in world history, since it had widespread repercussions throughout the East and did more than any other single factor to stimulate the new spirit of oriental nationalism.

But the expansion of Western power and culture in the eighteenth and nineteenth centuries was not confined to the East. In many respects it was the Western development which was the most important, for nothing altered the balance of world power and population more decisively than the growth of a new centre of Western culture across the Atlantic. This development was almost entirely the work of the eighteenth and nineteenth centuries. At the beginning of the eighteenth century the colonization of the North American continent had hardly begun, and the English population were confined to a narrow and discontinuous fringe of settlements along the Atlantic coast. But from the Peace of Utrecht (1713), a process of expansion began which continued without a break for two centuries, until the whole continent was occupied from sea to sea. The Revolution and the Civil War were mere episodes by comparison with this vast movement of population. Far more important was the coming of the steamship and the railway which increased the volume of immigration and transformed the movement from a British to a pan-European one, and made North America a crucible in which elements from every European country were fused into a new national unity.

Hence the ambivalence of the American tradition. For the American people became international in its composition without losing its strong sense of nationality and national patriotism; and at the same time, although it owed its existence to colonialism and was in fact the greatest of

all the European colonies, it possessed a conscious anti-
colonial ethos which leads Americans to sympathize with
the peoples of the East (especially perhaps with the Indians
and Indonesians) in their resistance to Western (European)
influences. In South America and Mexico the pattern of
colonialism is very different; there the work of colonization
was carried out in the previous periods—and especially the
sixteenth century—and it left a large native population in
existence, so that the situation in Central America and the
Andean republics resembles that of the European colonies
in Asia and Africa rather than that of the United States.
Only in the Argentine and South Brazil are conditions favourable to a development of the North American type. In
the British dominions, on the other hand, in Canada and
Australia and New Zealand, the social pattern is similar to
that of the U.S.A., although the scale of development has
been much smaller and the new societies are less international in composition. Yet they too have contributed to the
change in the axis of world power, by the establishment of
centres of Western culture in the Pacific and the Antipodes.

To sum up: this period of two centuries saw the irremedi-
able decline of the three great oriental empires owing to
their own internal weakness rather than to direct pressure
from the West. But the power vacuum thus created was
filled by the growth of Western economic and naval and
military power. The most important result of this process
was not the building of the colonial empires, important as
these were, but the creation of a world-wide network of
communications and commercial relations based on Western maritime power and on an international system of credit

and finance. The banker, the merchant, the consul, the shipper, the engineer, the planter and the colonist formed the links of a continuous chain extending from London and New York to the islands of the Pacific, the rivers of China and the rice fields of India and Burma. The maintenance of this chain involved the charting and policing of the seven seas, the suppression of piracy and the slave trade and the enforcement of Western commercial law in Asiatic communities. It was essentially a cosmopolitan system based on the economic liberalism of Adam Smith and the English economists, and it involved the opening of the world not only to the Western trader, but also to the explorer, the scientist and the missionary. The great age of expansion during the nineteenth century was the golden age of the individual pioneer, naturalists like Darwin and Wallace and Fortune, explorers like Barth and Lander and Caillet, orientalists like Lane and Hodgson and Burton, missionaries like Livingstone and Huc and Judson.

The total impact of the West on the East during this period is incalculable, since it was diffused through a thousand different channels, and the rivalry and competition between the different European powers multiplied the opportunities of infiltration. Only the most remote and thinly peopled regions of the world—Tibet, Arabia and Mongolia —were able to maintain their isolation, and even in these cases the attempt to exclude Western influence stimulated the efforts of Western explorers to break through the curtain. Of course there have always been intrepid travellers in the East as well as the West—Chinese monks in ancient India, Arab merchants in medieval Russia and Africa, et

cetera—but it was only in the Western expansion that exploration was literally world-wide and that every drop of
knowledge was collected and canalized by academies and
learned institutions into one vast river of universal knowledge which fertilized every province of culture.

Nor should the predominantly economic and capitalist
character of this movement of Western expansion lead us
to ignore its spiritual aspects. The religious, scientific and
humanitarian motives and factors in the movement were all
of them important.

The remarkable cultural work of the Catholic missionaries in the East continued into the early part of this period.
Indeed it was during the eighteenth century that the Jesuits
did most to spread the knowledge of Chinese culture and
history in Europe. Nevertheless the eighteenth century was
a period of decline and even of catastrophe for the Catholic
missions. The controversy on the Chinese rites resulted in
the formal prohibition of the preaching of Christianity in
China. Still more disastrous for the missions, alike in Asia
and elsewhere, was the suppression of the Jesuits by the
Papacy in 1773, and this was soon followed by the French
Revolution, which practically put an end to Catholic missionary activity for a generation. The discouragement and
defeatism which was caused by these events finds expression
in the "Letters on the State of Christianity in India," which
the Abbé Dubois published after his return to Europe in
1823 from a mission that had lasted for thirty years, and in
which he regards the conversion of the higher castes of
Hinduism as a hopeless task. Nevertheless the nineteenth
century saw a remarkable and world-wide revival of mis-

sionary activity, so that, as we have seen, the American historian of Christian Missions, Professor Latourette, has entitled it "The Great Century." The new movement, which began in the last decade of the eighteenth century, was Protestant in origin and was especially associated with the pietist sects—Moravian, Baptist and Wesleyan, and with the Evangelical movement in the Church of England. Unlike the earlier Jesuit movement, the new missionaries made no attempt to adapt themselves to oriental culture. In fact they were frankly and naively Western in their approach, denouncing native culture as tainted with heathenism, and advocating Western ideas, Western education and Western trade.[2] It was through their agency that the influence of Western culture first reached the mind of the Eastern peoples. It was not always a very high type of culture, and with some eminent exceptions, it did not reach the most highly educated representatives of oriental culture—the Brahmins, the Confucian scholars and the Arab and Persian "ulama." But it promoted the meeting of East and West on a middle ground, between Europeans and Asiatics who neither of them belonged to the ruling caste in their respective communities. Most of the missionaries were of humble origins. The great pioneer in India, William Carey (1761–1834), who did more than any man of his generation for the study of Indian languages, was a village shoemaker from Northamptonshire, Marshman was the son of a weaver, Morrison (1782–1834), the first Protestant missionary to China, had been a bootmaker. Yet it was these men and others like them who

[2] In this last respect Livingstone's Travels and Journals are very instructive, since he regards the missionary and the trader as allies through whose co-operation alone the slave trade can be suppressed.

did far more than the scholars and the administrators to introduce Western education into the East and to promote the study of oriental languages.

This Protestant missionary movement was followed in the course of the nineteenth century by a great revival of Catholic missions, which was supported by the restoration of the Jesuits and the foundation of new missionary orders, most of them French in origin and recruitment. But on the whole it was the Protestant missionaries, especially in China and India, who had the greatest educational influence, since it was they who identified themselves most completely with Western cultural views. The Catholics concentrated their energies on building strong local Christian communities, while the Protestants favoured broadcast propaganda by preaching, literature and education designed to reach the widest possible public.

This approach was especially important in China, where the missionaries for a long time provided the only access to Western knowledge, as we see from the outstanding case of Sun Yat-sen himself. He received his early education at Bishop's College in Honolulu and at Hong Kong, where he became a Christian. He was afterwards trained as a doctor at the American hospital at Canton, and at the London Missionary Society's medical school at Hong Kong. Thus his whole career was moulded by missionary influences, and it was as a Christian that he began his campaign for the political reform of China on Western democratic lines.

In fact the whole movement of reform in the later nineteenth century, which was the forerunner of the Chinese Revolution, was steeped in missionary influences. The most influential thinker and writer of that movement, Liang Ch'i-Ch'ao, acted for years as the secretary of the Welsh missionary, Timothy Richards, who had many friends among Chinese intellectuals, and exerted great influence in educational matters. And still earlier, an American missionary, W. H. P. Martin, had been appointed head of the Tung Wen Kuan College which had been founded in 1862, to train the candidates for the foreign service. And these are only the most outstanding examples of a large class that included learned sinologists like James Legge and Alexander Wylie, as well as medical missionaries and popularizers of Western science.

Elsewhere in Asia, the influence of the missionaries was not so great, since in Japan the impetus to change came from the government itself, and in India it was the influence of the official system of Western education that was most important. Yet there also the missionaries continued to play an important part alike in the higher education[3] and in popular education. It was the missionaries above all who attacked the fundamental social problem of India—the question of caste—and who were the first to attempt to raise the social and intellectual position of the Untouchables.

But it is obvious that in spite of the agreement between the ideals of the Protestant missionaries, and the liberal gospel of free trade and social progress, there was an obvious contradiction between Christian ideals and the realities of Western commercial exploitation. The conflict was sharpest

[3] It is significant that even today so prominent a Hindu leader as Sardar Panikkar should have received a Christian education—first in a C.M.S. High School, and then at St. Paul's School and at the Madras Christian College.

in the less civilized areas, as in Africa and the Pacific.[4] But it was sufficiently evident in Indonesia, where the tradition of economic exploitation was deeply rooted, and in China, where the Europeans were identified with the opium trade and the coolie traffic. The idea of imperialism is nothing new in Asia, where political oppression has been as inevitable as war and famine and disease. But commercial exploitation and the privileged position of the foreign merchant and money lender is alien to their traditions and arouses a strong moral resistance. The ruthless exploitation of their economic opportunities by the English traders and bankers in India in the eighteenth century and by Western traders in China and elsewhere in the following period did more than anything else to sow the seeds of the anti-Western sentiment which was ultimately to become a dominant factor in the relations of East and West.

[4] There is a good picture of the relations of traders and missionaries drawn from life in R. L. Stevenson's little masterpiece "The Beach of Falesa."

10

The Rise of Oriental Nationalism

THE development of the nationalist movements in Asia and Africa is one of the most momentous features of the present period. During the last ten years it has changed the face of the world and altered the balance of world power. Its consequences affect not only the powers like Britain and France and the Netherlands, whose political and colonial interests are directly threatened, but every Western power and not least the United States. It means nothing less than the sudden awakening to political consciousness of the greater part of the human race, both the peoples which have been for centuries passive spectators, like the Indians and the Chinese, and those, like the Negro peoples of Africa, who have up to now remained almost totally unconscious of the world forces on which their fate depended. Now they are all plunging into the political arena with intense excitement and unlimited self-confidence and hope. The stately quadrille of the old European diplomacy has been converted into a shouting match between hundreds of peoples who have only just realized their own identity and each other's existence. The victorious Western powers in 1945 asked for One World and they have got it with a vengeance, and no one can foretell what the results will be.

It is perhaps difficult for us to realize the importance of what is happening. The national state and the concept of nationality have been familiar to us in the West for centuries, but in Asia during the past, nationality and even the State as we know it hardly existed. There was kingship and empire, and the ideal of a universal monarchy had existed ever since the days of the Persian King of Kings and even back to Sargon of Akkad. When the western European nations were acquiring political form the Asian world was dominated by a real world monarchy, the Mongol Empire which ruled from the Pacific to the Black Sea. In later times the oriental world was dominated by three great empires, the Turkish Empire in the Near East, the Mogul Empire in India, and the Chinese Empire in the Far East; but none of these were political societies of the same type as the Western nation states are. They were far removed from the interests and anxieties of the ordinary man, whom one cannot even call a citizen. The most important functions of the modern Western State were performed by other social institutions; by the sub-caste in India, by the family and clan in China and by the tribe or religious community, or *millet,* in the Turkish Empire. Politics was in theory the business of kings and in practice was often an affair of intrigues by the eunuchs of the court or conspiracies by mercenary soldiers. The idea of the ordinary man's having anything to do with politics was unheard of and when the first nationalists in the East tried to make their voices heard they paid for it with their heads. Nothing is more instructive than the terms of the sentence of death, in 1859, on Yoshida Torajiro or Shoin, the Japanese nationalist, whose story was told long ago by R. L. Stevenson. The text of the sentence is as follows:[1]

Item. He tried to go to America.

Item. He advised the Government on central defence while in jail.

Item. He opposed the hereditary succession to office and favoured the selection of able men by popular vote.

Item. He planned to give his opinion regarding foreigners to the Bakufu.

Item. He did such things while in domiciliary confinement, thus showing great disrespect for high officials.

The emergence of the Asiatic peoples from this state of total subservience to a state of political consciousness, self-determination and full citizenship has been the great mission of oriental nationalism and that is why it arouses such intense emotional reaction. For as President Sukarno said recently, "For us nationalism is everything. Though nationalism in the West may be an out-of-date doctrine for many, for us in Asia and Africa it is the mainspring of our efforts."

No doubt oriental and African nationalism is itself of Western origin, like so much else—like democracy and representative government, engineering and sanitation, newspapers and popular education, broadcasting and atom bombs. But whereas in Europe nationalism developed gradually out

[1] As quoted by G. B. Sansom, *The Western World and Japan* (London, Cresset Press, Ltd.; New York, Knopf, 1950), p. 289.

of the traditional Western system of small highly-organized
political units, who all shared the same culture and the same
religious and moral traditions, in Asia and Africa it came
into a world of empires and civilizations which had followed
their own ways of life for thousands of years and which were
for all practical purposes so many distinct and separate
worlds. In these different worlds nationalism assumes new
forms. In some cases, as in India and China, the nation is
identified with the civilization, though the civilization may
be larger than the whole of Western Europe; in other cases,
as in Africa, the nation may be identified with the tribe, as
with the Kikuyu, or else with the inhabitants of a territory
which has recently possessed a common administration,
though a foreign one. Again, in the Islamic countries nationalism operates on two planes and represents both a common pan-Arab or pan-Islamic unity and territorial units like
Syria or Irak.

But everywhere among the great civilizations of the East
and the tribal societies of Africa, the new nationalist movement possesses certain common characteristics—it is anti-
foreign and, especially, anti-Western and anti-colonial, and
it is democratic in the sense that it appeals to the sentiment
of the broad mass of the common people and bases itself
on the principles of the self-determination of peoples and
the rights of man.

In fact, one may say that it is only through the oriental
nationalist movement that Western democratic ideas have
penetrated the East, and thus oriental nationalism, though
apparently anti-European, has in fact been the chief agent
of the diffusion of European ideas. No doubt in the nine-

teenth century liberal-democratic ideas had already begun to affect the oriental world, especially in India and Japan and in the Near East, but they were confined to a small elite and though they made some very distinguished converts, they aroused considerable popular antagonism. It was only in their militant nationalist form that the new ideas gained a wide measure of popular support and became a revolutionary force. But as a revolutionary force they proved even more effective against the old oriental order than against Western Imperialism. It was the nationalists who destroyed the Khalifate, and the Chinese monarchy, which was the most ancient political institution in the world. And this was one of the greatest paradoxes of recent history, since both these institutions had always been regarded as the chief bulwarks of Asiatic resistance to Western influence, and at the very moment when the Turkish nationalists were destroying the Khalifate, the Indian Moslems were organizing a great campaign against the British Empire in its defence.

Consequently oriental nationalism does not mean, as one might suppose, a reaction in defence of traditional oriental culture; on the contrary it means the adoption or appropriation by the Eastern peoples of Western culture. It stands for a new way of life which is as a rule secularist and antitraditional. The communist states are the most extreme example of this, since they deliberately aim at rebuilding the whole social edifice on the basis of an ideology which originated in London in the Victorian age, and was developed down to the smallest detail in twentieth-century Russia. But the same occidentalizing tendency is to be seen in purely nationalist states which are not in any way contaminated by communist ideology. Thus, the introduction of the new order in Turkey was marked by the systematic secularization of the Turkish state and culture—the abolition of Islam as the state religion, the introduction of a new legal code based on European models and the substitution of the Latin alphabet for the Arabic script.

When one considers the strength of the forces that these movements had to contend with—the organized political and economic power of the European world on the one hand, and the age-long influence of religion and custom and law on the other—their success seems almost miraculous. There were, however, two great factors in their favour. In the first place, the ordinary man had become convinced of the efficacy of Western techniques. He had learnt the lesson in the hard school of war. Even the most conservative, who remained entirely convinced of the superiority of oriental religion and culture, could not shut their eyes to the military and economic power of the West, and at a very early date they recognized that it was necessary to learn the secrets of Western technical efficiency if they were to survive.

To do this they had to accept some degree of Western education. But it proved impossible to limit education to purely technical subjects. Western techniques were inseparable from Western ideas, and the students who were trained in Europe and America or under Western teachers became converts to the Western way of life, and apostles of Western social and political ideas. Thus there grew up all over the East, and at a later period in Africa also, a new educated class which was entirely alienated from the old learned classes—the Confucian scholars in China, the Brahmins in

India and the Ulema in Islam—and which shared the culture of the student class of the West and especially of the liberal and revolutionary intelligentsia.

It was this new class that created the modern nationalist movement in the East. Their indoctrination with Western ideas only made them more determined to assert their equality with the European and to claim the right to national self-determination. As the conservatives had been ready to accept Western aims and Western military methods to defend themselves against the West, so the new nationalist intelligentsia were prepared to accept Western education, Western ideas and the whole apparatus of Western culture in order to shake off their material dependence on the West and to take part on equal terms in the social and intellectual life of the modern world.

Thus oriental nationalism is essentially an educational movement. It had its origin in the student class which had an unbounded faith in the value of Western education, and its progress involves a vast movement of re-education which aims at converting the illiterate peasant masses of Asia into fully conscious citizens of the modern democratic state. It is in this field that the success of the nationalists has been most remarkable. They have not succeeded as yet in modernizing the economy of the Asiatic peoples, nor have they made very marked progress in raising the standard of life of the peasant. But they have made revolutionary changes in the sphere of popular education and in combating illiteracy. Fifty years ago popular education hardly existed in Asia; today it is almost universal, at least in theory. And all this has been accompanied by an awakening of the mind of the masses, which is changing the whole spirit of oriental culture. It is no longer possible to speak of the Unchanging East, for the East is being transformed under our eyes as rapidly as—perhaps even more rapidly than—Europe was changed during the Industrial Revolution. This is the great achievement of oriental nationalism, and it is not limited to a single class or country, but affects the whole of Asia and is rapidly extending to Africa as well. Hence the paradox that nationalism is an international movement; international not only in its external influence, but also in its social and ideological constitution. While the old cultures of the East were so highly differentiated that they appear as separate worlds, the new nationalist movements are everywhere the same. They have the same kind of leaders drawn from the same student class, which is almost an international one; they are embodied in the same type of political parties, they use the same types of propaganda, and they advocate similar programmes of social reform and the same modern type of universal compulsory education. No doubt this internationalism is superficial, since it is confined to the educated minorities. But since these minorities are the politically active section of the population and since they are constantly increasing owing to the spread of education and the intensification of nationalist propaganda, it would be very unwise to underestimate its importance. Although it is hardly possible to conceive of an United States of Asia, there is a growing sense of international community and a growing desire for closer relations between the Asiatic and African peoples, and the Bandung conference or conferences mark an important step towards the realization of this community.

The force behind this new international community is not unity of culture, since there is no common Asiatic culture, still less a common Afro-Asian one. Neither is it a common political ideology, since it includes both Communist and anti-Communist parties and states. In a sense it is a racialist movement, but it represents no common racial unity; rather is it an anti-racialist movement, which represents the common reaction of all the non-European peoples against the political power, the economic privilege and the racial prejudice of Western Europeans and Americans. This racial element in the nationalist movement is of course greatly intensified by the colour question and the existence of a colour bar in certain countries. It is easy enough to understand this in the United States and the West Indies and South and East Africa, where white men and Negroes are brought into close relations within a single society which is dominated by the white man. At first sight, however, it seems difficult to see what bearing it has on Asiatic nationalism, where the conditions are totally different and where language and religion play a much greater part than complexion in determining men's social status and affiliation, and where the differences of colour within a single state are often greater than those between some Asiatics and some Europeans. Moreover, in Asia the boot is on the other foot, since the Arabs and the high-caste Indian have always been convinced of their racial superiority to the European, while the Chinese have always possessed a sense of cultural superiority which is infinitely stronger than anything that has ever been known in Europe.

The fact remains, however, that the Asiatic has suffered

in the past from the arrogance and bad manners or tactlessness of the European trader and colonist and administrator, and that this experience has made him intensely resentful of all Western claims to superiority and very sympathetic to the Africans and the American Negroes who suffer from social discrimination on purely racial grounds.

There is a danger that the growing internationalism of the East may not make for world peace but may only deepen the breach between East and West, and unite the Asian and African peoples in a common front against the West. We see the first fruits of this movement in the Bandung Conference of 1955, and in the growing tendency of the Arab peoples to look to Russia and China for support against the West.

But how far can this movement go without endangering the independence of the nationalist movements themselves? So long as the West still retains the vestiges of its economic and political power in Asia and Africa, Soviet imperialism and oriental nationalism can co-operate in an anti-colonialist policy. But the moment the West withdraws from the East, the new peoples of the East will find themselves faced with a new imperialism which may prove much more formidable than that which has been displaced. Even at the present time there is a growing contradiction between the ideologies and cultures of the new "people's democracies" of China and the satellite states of the Soviet world, and the medieval theocratic monarchies of Saudi Arabia and the Yemen, which owe their power and importance to the American oil companies; and the success of the present regime in Egypt depends on maintaining a delicate balance between the two.

Above all we must remember that all the new nationalist and Communist parties have their own oppositions to contend with, and these oppositions are more truly nationalist —that is to say more representative of the national traditions of their cultures—than are the dominant parties. Thus, behind the dominant parties, which are modernist, secularist and occidentalist, we find a series of opposition parties which are devoted to the intransigent defence of cultural and religious tradition. In India there is the Mahasabha, the representative of orthodox Hinduism, which was the chief opponent of the Congress Party, as well as a number of Communal national movements like that of the Sikhs. In Pakistan there is the Islamic Party, which utterly rejects the compromise with the secularism which is the official policy of the present regime. In Egypt there is the Muslim Brotherhood, which has been forcibly suppressed by Colonel Nasser's government, and in Indonesia there have been similar movements which have led to civil war.

It is more difficult to speak of such movements in the Communist territories, not merely because they have been ruthlessly repressed, but even more because the whole force of the totalitarian propaganda system is directed to minimizing and misinterpreting them. From the beginning Soviet Communism recognized the importance of the nationalities and did all it could to avoid the mistakes of the Tzarist government, and to win over the national minorities to the Revolution. To this end it established the numerous Constituent National Republics and Autonomous Regions which make up the U.S.S.R., and granted very liberal linguistic and cultural rights to every national group. At the same time the nominal rights of the national republics to complete auton-

omy and self-determination were contradicted by the strict
monopoly of power by the local Communist parties, so that
any genuine opposition or any real assertion of nationalist
views was stigmatized as counter-revolutionary, reactionary
and anti-democratic, and was ruthlessly suppressed. In spite
of this there has been no lack of nationalist resistance movements, and whole tribes and peoples have been decimated,
deported and even destroyed.

Thus the Soviet policy to nationalism consists of two
contradictory elements: on the one hand an ultra-liberal,
theoretical attitude to cultural autonomy; on the other, an
Assyrian ruthlessness against any assertion of ideological or
political independence. But these two elements are not so
contradictory as they appear at first sight. For the larger
the number of national minority groups that are officially
recognized, the greater is the disproportion between each of
them and the vast monolithic unity of the Great Russian
people and of the Russian Soviet Republic which embraces
seventy-seven per cent or more of the total territory. As
against this great unity of a hundred million Russians, Soviet
ethnologists recognize the existence of one hundred and
sixty-eight other nationalities in the Union. Most of these
are Asiatic nationalities, but even the most important of
them, like the Uzbeks or the Kazaks, only number between
three and five million apiece. Yet for all that the Turkish
peoples of Central Asia possess a very strong sense of common racial and historical tradition, which under more favourable circumstances might well have created a nation.
This finds literary expression in the work of the Kazak poet,
Maghjan Jumbay of Yedisu, for though he took a leading

part in the long war of resistance of the Kazaks against the Soviets, he is not so much concerned with the practical issue of Kazak political freedom, as with the cause of the Turkish peoples in general. He writes of

The sacred Issik Kol, on which the first Turk
Born of the grey wolf, saw the light of the world.
The two rivers, Jaihun and Saihun
And between them the sacred graves of the ancestors.
The great mountains of Turan, Khan Tengri reaching to heaven;
Look now to the mountains and think how the Turks suffer in bondage.[2]

And it is remarkable that though the movement of resistance to Russia in Central Asia was mainly inspired by strict Islamic orthodoxy, like some of the other opposition movements and parties I have discussed, the poet himself looks for something different—some new religious leader who will bring salvation to the Turks:

Thou gavest to every land,
To the poor Arabia, nurse of camels,
A prophet to show the way and a holy book,
But to us Turks this grace has not been given,
We have followed prophets from divers lands
And set our faith in holy words,
But the way has not been shown us.
Lord, send us a prophet to show us that way.[3]

This Messianic appeal is not a mere literary device on the

[2] Translated by O. K. Caroe, *The Soviet Empire* (London, Macmillan; New York, St. Martin's Press, 1953), p. 227.
[3] *Ibid.*, p. 228.

part of a modern nationalist man of letters. For already a generation before the poet appealed to the Turks of Anatolia to go back in spirit to the Altai and "mount the golden throne of their forefathers," the primitive pagan Turks of the Altai had actually produced a prophet who announced the imminent return to earth of the last descendant of Chinghiz Khan, who would deliver the Turks from Russian oppression and unite them in a new kingdom. It was called the religion of the White Burkhan and was quickly repressed by the Russians. But it is extremely doubtful whether Maghjan Jumbay had ever heard of it.

Similar movements are to be found all over the world. They were especially strong in North America during the eighteenth and nineteenth centuries and are represented today in the so-called Cargo cults of New Guinea. But they are not confined to primitive peoples, for the great T'ai P'ing movement which convulsed China in the nineteenth century, and almost led to the downfall of the Empire, belonged to the same class of movement.

Now, at first sight there seems little in common between these Messianic social movements, which the ethnologists term nativistic, and the nationalisms which I discussed in the first part of this essay. For the latter are secular and political and modernist, while the former are reactionary and religious and irrational. They look back to an imaginary golden age of native culture, while the latter look forward to a social Utopia in the future. Yet the difference is not as great as it seems. Every revolutionary movement has a Messianic element. Communism itself is a secular Messianism, which announces the judgment of the Capitalist world and the coming of a new order of social justice. The nativistic movements are more religious and less political than the nationalist ones, because they answer to the situation of peoples who have no opportunity of political action and who are faced with an alien culture which is overwhelmingly strong, as was the case with the Indians of the Plains in the nineteenth century. At the present time, however, we are witnessing the appearance of new movements like the Mau Mau movement in Kenya, which are intermediate between the two types—which are at once nationalist and nativistic, and which combine a political programme with an appeal to irrational motives and forces.

And we may ask whether such a combination of elements is not to be seen nearer home in such movements as National Socialism in Germany, which has made a more violent impact on the world than any of the more orthodox forms of political nationalism.

The defeat of Hitlerism does not mean that we have seen the last of such movements. In our modern democratic world irrational forces lie very near the surface, and their sudden eruption under the impulse of nationalist or revolutionary ideologies is the greatest of all the dangers that threaten the modern world. The fact that oriental nationalism has awakened the world and torn it loose from its old moorings in tradition and custom does not necessarily make for peace. On the contrary, it makes it more inflammable and more exposed to the influence of sudden irrational mass movements.

It is at this point that the need for a reassertion of Christian principles becomes evident. Nationalism is essentially a force of division. It contains no universal principle of unity or international order. If the world is left to the unrestricted development of nationalistic movements, it will become a Babel of people who not only speak different tongues, but follow different laws and seek divergent ends. As a means of evoking common loyalty and common action within a single society, there is no denying the value and efficiency of nationalism. But as an ultimate principle of human action, it is morally inadequate and socially destructive. Left to itself, it becomes a form of mass egotism and self-idolatry which is the enemy of God and man. This has always been realized in some degree by the great civilizations of the past. All of them have admitted the existence of a higher law above that of the tribe and the nation, and consequently subordinated national interest and political power to the higher spiritual values which are derived from this source. On this point there is a consensus of principle which unites all the world religions and all the great civilizations of the past alike in the East and the West. All agree that the social order does not exist merely to serve men's interests and passions. It is the expression of a sacred order by which human action is conformed to the order of heaven and the eternal law of divine justice.

Now, in so far as nationalism denies this principle and sets up the nation and the national State as the final object of man's allegiance, it represents the most retrograde movement that the world has ever seen, since it means a denial of the great central truth on which civilization was founded, and a return to the pagan idolatries of tribal barbarism.

We cannot ignore the serious nature of this challenge, for

the new barbarism which results from total nationalism is a fact of contemporary history and of our own experience. And in order that we should have no excuse for shutting our eyes to its significance, the first thing that the totalitarian, national State did was to set about the extermination of the very people which had denounced the idolatry of the Gentiles and whose historic mission it was to assert the unity and sovereignty of God. The catastrophic events of the last thirty years have shown us two things—first that there is no limit to man's powers of destructiveness, and secondly that nothing could be more dangerous than to leave these powers at the mercy of national ambition and resentment.

The changes in the conditions of war and world power make it more important than ever before to re-establish the traditional religious and moral limits in man's social activities, and to make the nations conscious of their responsibilities to God and their neighbour. The secular forms of international organization cannot help us, for they depend either on the absolutism of the totalitarian State, as with Communism, or on the divided wills of the conflicting nationalisms themselves, as in the case of democratic internationalism. The only solution is to be found in the restoration of the traditional religious sanctions; the acceptance by nations as well as by individuals of a transcendent authority which provides a common norm of right action to which every nation and every individual must conform.

This belief in the Law of Nature and the Law of God is so ancient and so universal that it has been taken for granted and dismissed as a platitude, or else misinterpreted in accordance with the philosophical fashions of the moment, and thus denied. Today, however, it has become the vital principle on which the survival of civilization, and indeed of humanity, depends.

But it may be objected that politics are not the only source of national conflict. Even if religion could be restored to its ancient position in and above the State, can we be sure that this would lead to world peace? Is it not possible that conflicts would be intensified by the injection of religious intolerance? Above all, are not the fundamental differences between Eastern and Western civilizations of a religious nature, so that the partial degree of unity that the modern world has attained has been due to its secularization and to the substitution of science for theology as the basis of cultural unity?

It must be admitted that there is a real difficulty here. In the past religion has been the cause or the pretext of countless wars and persecutions, and faith in God has not always led to peace and goodwill among men. Nor are these things confined to the past. For the fearful outburst of violence and mass killing which followed the withdrawal of the British from India and the achievement of national independence was religious rather than political in origin, and the tragedy reached its climax when the man who stood before all others for the cause of Indian nationalism fell a victim at the age of seventy-eight to the religious extremism of his own people.

It has been said that "Gandhi offered his life blood as a living oblation to the liquidation of communalism in the social relations of the Indian people," and his attitude in those last months far transcended any mere political nationalism. It was religious in the highest sense of the word. At the same time it is difficult to deny that he was himself responsible in some degree for these catastrophic events, since he did more than anyone else to enlist the religious instincts of the masses in the cause of nationalism and thus to awaken the irrational forces to which he himself fell a victim.

For beneath the surface of the oriental nationalist movements, which are political, secular and democratic, there are the age-old differences of culture and religion and race which exercise a profound unconscious influence on the thought and behaviour of the masses. These differences can be ignored by the politicians as long as they are dealing with one another, since the politically active classes are for the most part made up of men and women who have been more or less deeply influenced by Western education, who all speak the same language and think in the same categories. But when we come to the peoples themselves this is no longer the case; there is no common language, and though there are common values, these values are bound up with traditions and institutions which have no common ground in history and social experience.

This is the fundamental problem that Christianity has to face. The Christian Church has a divine mission to all peoples, alike of East and West. She must speak to all nations so that as at Pentecost each may "hear in his own language the wonderful works of God." But how is it possible for her to speak to the peoples of Asia and Africa when these are separated from the Christian world by a wall or a number of walls that have been built up by thousands of years of cultural and religious history? It is not just a question of different nations, but of different *worlds of nations*. This is the most difficult of all questions, since it has hitherto proved an insurmountable obstacle to the ecumenical development of the Christian Faith, and has confined Christianity to one very limited portion of the human race. But it is a problem that has got to be faced, and I will try to deal with it in the following chapter.

11

Christianity and the Oriental Cultures

AT THE end of the previous chapter I distinguished between the question of oriental nationalism and that of oriental culture. The two questions are apt to be confused, naturally enough under the present circumstances, when the conflict between East and West is always seen as an international political issue. But oriental nationalism is a very recent phenomenon, and from the historical point of view the great barrier between East and West has not been due to nationalist sentiment, but to religion and culture. In the East, as in the medieval West, man's primary and fundamental allegiance was not to his nation, but to his religion, and men thought of themselves as Muslims or Hindus or Buddhists or Sikhs, rather than Egyptians or Syrians or Indians or Indonesians. The one great exception is China, and China was not a nation but a civilization—and a civilization of a unique and very exclusive character which had been identified for thousands of years with a particular tradition of thought, and distinctive ideals of moral behaviour.

Modern nationalism has brought the East nearer to the West than ever before; its success has been due to its assimilation of Western culture, and its leaders have been that part of the population which has been most deeply influenced by modern Western ideas; above all, the class of students who have studied in Western schools and universities and who use English or French as their second language. But behind this world of the new oriental intelligentsia, there is the older world of the traditional religious cultures whose roots reach back to the most remote past. Although their influence has been steadily decreasing for the last century or two, they still mould the minds and lives of their members down to the smallest details of behaviour, and even the Westernized minorities which have revolted against the tyranny of tradition and custom keep a profound bond with them which goes far deeper than any conscious loyalty, like the bond of the child with his mother's womb.

Thus, as I said previously, when we speak of the East we are not merely speaking of a number of different nationalities but of a number of different worlds of peoples, each of which is separated from the others by thousands of years of civilization. For thousands of years the nations have travelled on different roads, and these roads have tended to diverge ever further in the course of ages. Above all, these different roads have been different approaches to reality and different ways of religious worship and doctrine. For religion in the East is not a private matter for the individual conscience, as in the modern Western world, where men of different religions and sects can share the same culture and society without any sense of strain or conflict. The religions of the East are sacred orders or liturgical cultures in which every detail of behaviour has a religious significance, so that it is possible to tell what a man's religion is by the way he eats his dinner or ties his dress.

This is most obvious in the case of Hinduism, which is an immense and intricate hierarchy of hereditary religious societies, each governed by its own religious laws and rites, and all subordinated to the highest caste of the hereditary priesthood, which preserved the monopoly of learning and ritual and legal knowledge. Thus the whole social system and the social function of the individual is of divine right and is hedged round with religious sanctions and rites. The position of the State is unimportant, since the hereditary religious societies and castes transcend the State and it is their law, not that of the State, which rules men's daily lives.

In contrast to this we have the case of China, which was the most secular in spirit of all the great civilizations and owed its unity not to a religion but to an empire, the historical origin of which is older than that of Rome, while its tradition goes back further still into the mist of prehistoric legend. Nevertheless the civilization of ancient China was also a sacred order—a liturgical civilization founded on the sacred rites—and demanded the total subordination of the individual to the sacred traditions that had been handed down from antiquity. When we consider the great ceremony that was carried out without a break by the Emperors at the Altar of Heaven and the constant emphasis of the State ritual on the dependence of the Empire on the Mandate of Heaven, it is impossible to describe ancient Chinese culture as secular. At the same time it is not religious in our sense of the word. It has a certain resemblance to the official religion of the Roman Empire in the Augustan age.

In the case of Islam, on the other hand, the religious character of the culture is much easier for us to understand, since its theological background has much in common with that of Catholicism. The Moslem theologians lay down in categorical terms that the purpose of human life is the service of God (*Ibâda*), that Moslem society is a community expressly constituted to fulfill this purpose, and that it is the function of the State to safeguard the community in carrying out its liturgical mission both against the external enemy by the conquest of the unbelievers and against internal enemies by defending it against the perils of heresy and schism. There is no room for nationalism, since all the Moslems are brothers; and there is no room for political democracy, since Islam is a theocracy, and both the religious community and the political State exist only to assert the divine authority and to carry out the divine law.

These three worlds of culture were entirely diverse and incommensurable both in thought and in social institutions. But owing to the absence of nationalism they possessed a greater degree of internal organic unity than Western civilization. Ancient China was a single society in every sense of the word; ancient India possessed social uniformity without political unity, and Islam was a true and full spiritual community and in theory a single universal state, although it ultimately came to be divided among a number of different kingdoms which nominally recognized the universal authority of the Khalifate, somewhat as the later German and Italian principalities recognized the authority of the Holy Roman Empire.

These great unities are so impressive by their antiquity

and monolithic stability that they have given rise to the idea of the "unchanging East" and of the stationary and unprogressive character of oriental culture. But in the past they were all growing organisms and enjoyed their periods of expansion and progress. The influence of Chinese culture spread all over the Far East, eastwards to Korea and Japan, westwards into Central Asia and south to Indo-China. So, too, Indian culture underwent a great movement of expansion in antiquity, and above all in the early Middle Ages, and its sphere of influence extended far to the south and east to Ceylon and Cambodia and Champa and Java, as well as northward to Tibet and Central Asia. It was this outer zone of Indian culture that provided the most favourable conditions for the expansion of Buddhism, which continued to develop there after it had failed to maintain itself in India, somewhat as Christianity continued to spread in Western Europe after it had begun to decline in Syria and the Near East. Indeed it may be argued that these outer lands of Indian culture—the Buddhist world—should be reckoned as a fourth great oriental unity which forms an intermediate civilization between those of India and China.

But the most striking example of the expansion of oriental culture is to be seen in the case of Islam, which has continued to expand from its original centre in Arabia until it has spread from the Atlantic to the Pacific and from the Volga and the Irtish to the Zambesi and the Niger. Nor can we say that this expansion is a thing of the past; Islam is still advancing in Africa and may well become the dominant power in that continent.

Thus we must recognize that down to fairly recent times

it was the oriental cultures that were the main centres of world power and economic development and Christendom that was comparatively weak and poor and backward. It had been steadily pushed out of Asia and Africa by the advance of Islam, which was built on the ruins of an older Christian world. Even in Europe the situation was uncertain, since Spain and Sicily formed an integral part of the Islamic world in the early Middle Ages, Russia was incorporated in the Mongol world empire in the thirteenth century and the advance of the Ottoman Turks in southeast Europe extended the frontiers of Islam to the Danube and beyond.

Yet in spite of all this the last few centuries have seen a complete reversal of the situation: the rise of Western culture to a position of world hegemony, and a revolutionary process of change in Asia which has destroyed the old oriental empires and changed the character of the oriental cultures.

This process of world revolution—for it is nothing less—has passed through three successive phases:[1]

First of all there was the age of European discovery and colonization which gradually destroyed the separate worlds of the old cultures and created a global system of communication and trade under European control. Secondly, there was the breakdown of the old Asiatic empires owing to their inability to withstand the economic pressure of Western trade, the efficiency of Western technology and the influence of Western ideas.

Finally, the third phase saw the internal transformation

[1] The preceding three chapters in this section have dealt with these phases.

of oriental society by the spread of Western education and the rise of the nationalist movements, which represented at the same time a revolt against the West and the acceptance by the East of Western culture and political ideology. It is unnecessary to say more of this, as I have already discussed it at length in the foregoing chapter. But I cannot help drawing attention once more to the remarkable paradox that a movement which is rallying the peoples of Asia and Africa against the West is at the same time removing the cultural barriers between them and doing all in its power to diffuse Western education, Western science and Western political ideologies.

It is obvious that these great changes must have a profound influence on the relations between Christianity and the oriental peoples. But this involves a number of very complicated issues. For the results differ according to the circumstances of each culture and each nationality. In some cases Christianity may be regarded as the spiritual aspect of colonialism and consequently resisted as a foreign and anti-national phenomenon. In other cases Christianity is itself associated with national minorities, as in the Near East, where the national conflicts of the First World War and the succeeding period led to the wholesale destruction of the Armenian and Greek communities of Asia Minor and the Nestorian and Chaldean Churches of Western Mesopotamia and north-west Persia. On the other hand, in the case of the two greatest oriental civilizations, in India and China, Christian influences played a considerable part in the rise and development of the national movements. Since nationalism was the work of the new educated classes, the fact that the introduction of Western education into Asia was largely the work of Christian missionaries made for the growth of Christian influence on culture.

Above all, the nationalist revolutions have broken down the age-old barriers of tradition and custom which in the past made it so difficult for the Christian Church to speak directly to the hundred peoples of the East. The passing of the old order means the relaxation of the social pressures which often made religious change impossible, and the secular character of the new national states usually involves the acceptance of the principle of religious toleration. Thus in the East today Christianity finds itself faced with a similar situation to that which it had to encounter in the earliest period of its history. Then also the civilized world was passing through a period of revolutionary change. The civilizations of the ancient East—Egypt, Syria and Babylonia—which were of immemorial antiquity, had been subjugated by a Western movement of colonialism and imperialism, although they still retained their cultural identity and their old religious traditions. The resistance of Egypt to the influence of alien culture was just as strong as that of China or India to the West. Yet in spite of this the Christian Church, beginning in the great cosmopolitan cities of the Mediterranean, gradually spread through the whole of the Middle East, until by the fifth century the ancient religious culture of Egypt and Mesopotamia had been almost entirely replaced by Christianity.

Is such a change conceivable in Asia today? Certainly there is the same opportunity, since the advance of modern Western culture has broken down the barriers between the peoples in much the same way as the Roman Empire and the Hellenistic cosmopolitan culture broke down the barriers between the ancient cultures of the Near and Middle East two thousand years ago. But in the modern world the forces of religion are much weaker than they were in the ancient world and the forces making for secularization are far stronger. In the early centuries of the Christian era the world was aflame with a passionate interest in religion. It had lost its faith in the State and its interest in politics and had turned its eyes to the supernatural and to the hope of a divine saviour. To such a world the Christian Gospel came as the answer to a universally recognized need and it swept through the dry wood of the dead civilizations like a forest fire.

But today the situation is a very different one. There is the same discontent with the old order—the same thirst for something new. But the objectives are different: they are material and this-worldly: release from poverty and insecurity and admission to an equal status with the privileged classes and peoples.

Hence the appeal of Communism to the East, since Communism offers to the poor and underprivileged the hope of a kingdom of heaven on earth, while at the same time satisfying their resentment against the rich and powerful classes and nations that have exploited them.

Nevertheless, it is too early to judge. The old religions and cultures have been moulding men's lives and thoughts for thousands of years, Western influences and also Christian missionary activity have been at work for centuries— or at any rate for a century; but Communism is something entirely new—so new that it may have changed its character by the time that it has been fully adapted to the Asiatic environment. Although the East is in a state of fermentation and change, there is still an enormous mass to be leavened, and in many countries the process of change is still confined to the educated minority, which is naturally an urban class. But the vast majority of the people of Asia still live in their villages, and their lives are more remote from those of the nationalist or Communist intelligentsia than those of the latter are from the West.

A good example of this is to be seen in the recent study of an Indian village which was carried out by a team of Indian research workers headed by Dr. S. C. Dube. The village in question was in the State of Hyderabad and consequently, no doubt, more conservative than a comparable community in what was formerly British India. Nevertheless, it is only twenty-five miles from the capital of the state, which is one of the largest cities in India, and is connected with it by a regular bus service. Yet in spite of this many of the inhabitants had never heard of Mr. Nehru or Mahatma Gandhi, little was known of the movement for Indian independence, and national consciousness was vague. The real community was the village and the sub-caste, and "to the great bulk of the people caste-mythology was their only history."[2] Although Communism is active in the region and the Communist or rather Communist-supported candidate was successful in the first political election ever held (in 1951), its influence was very superficial and did not touch culture or

[2] S. C. Dube, *Indian Village* (London, Routledge & Kegan Paul; Ithaca, New York, Cornell University Press, 1955), p. 232.

religion. The religious life of the village goes on unchanged and it centres, not so much in the worship of the high gods of classical Hinduism, but in the local cult of the village goddesses—Pochamma, the goddess of smallpox, Mutyalamma, the goddess of chickenpox, Maisamma, the boundary goddess, and half-a-dozen more.

The modern world seems very remote from this little world, in which the craftsman still worships the instruments of his craft and where the Untouchables still perform religious dramas celebrating the exploits of the legendary founder of their sub-caste. But its influence is seeping in by a hundred channels and nothing can prevent its ultimate triumph.

The oriental world is being transformed before our eyes. But it is still not clear what the dominant force in the new culture will be. Will it be a drab secular materialism of the type that is so prevalent in the modern world, or a militant Communism, or some kind of reformed Hinduism such as is represented by the Arya Samaj? At first sight there seems little hope that Christianity will be the gainer or that there is any more chance of the Eastern world's becoming Christian than there was a hundred years ago. Nevertheless, though we cannot accept the cocksure historical determinism of the Marxians or the ambitious speculations of the philosophers of history, like Spengler and Toynbee, we believe as Christians that the hand of God is at work in history and that the great revolution of world culture that is taking place before our eyes is the instrument of divine purpose.

But we also have our part to play, and not the least important factor in this is the contribution that we make to the process of study and criticism and spiritual questioning upon which the peoples of the East are now engaged. They have been just as conscious as we are of the world crisis which is affecting civilization. For more than a century the impact of Western culture has made them re-examine the foundations of their civilization, so that they have been forced either to criticize or to justify their traditional way of life and the religious foundations on which it was based. In the past the influence of the Christian missions was here far from negligible. The whole history of the Indian national movement and the renaissance of Indian culture from the time of Ram Mohun Roy at the beginning of the nineteenth century to Mahatma Gandhi was penetrated through and through with specifically Christian as well as secular European influences. And the same is true of China, though in a lesser degree, since the founders of the nationalist movement were mission-educated and in some cases Christian, like Sun Yat-sen himself.

Now, the first effect of this impact was to produce reforming movements within the great religions of Asia—the Brahma Samaj and the Arya Samaj in India and the Ram Krishna Mission. On the basis of these movements and largely owing to Western influences there developed a generalized ideal of Eastern spirituality versus Western materialism: a theory that became prevalent in all the Asian civilizations and inspired the pan-Islamic ideology of Jamal ad-Din al-Afghani (1859–1897), Svami Vivekananda's vision of the world mission of Indian spirituality, and more recently in China Liang Sou-Ming's comparison of Eastern and Western civilization and their corresponding philosophies.

These views still exercise a good deal of influence, especially among the older generation, and have contributed to form that common Asian ideology which inspires the foreign policy of India and the Bandung Asian front. The whole subject has been recently reviewed in the remarkable study of Sardar Panikkar from which we have already quoted,[3] a book which not only takes a much more universal view than most books on oriental history, but which is almost unique in the space and attention that it devotes to the religious aspect of Western expansion in Asia and to the importance of Christian missionary action. He points out, as few non-Christian writers have done, "the unbroken religious urge of European expansion and the immense non-official and voluntary effort that it represented."[4]

In spite of this his final conclusions are altogether negative and unfavourable. He writes: "It will hardly be denied that in spite of the immense and sustained effort made by the churches with the support of the lay public in Europe and America, the attempt to conquer Asia for Christ has definitely failed. In China, where the effort was most concentrated, the collapse has been most complete. In India, the Christian church still exists—but mission work, except in the fields of education and medical services, is insignificant. Elsewhere, in Japan, Siam and Burma, the missionaries had no serious hopes, and with the assertion of national sentiments and the revival of oriental religions the prospects have become dimmer."[5]

Now if this view were correct it would mean that Chris-

[3] *Asia and Western Dominance.*
[4] *Ibid.*, p. 482.
[5] *Ibid.*, p. 454.

tianity had had its chance in Asia during the last centuries
and has lost it: so that the national revival of the peoples
of Asia involves the vindication of the ancient religions and
cultures of the East against the intrusion of Western colonial
power and Christian missionary influence. This, however, is
a gross simplification of a very complex problem. Western
colonialism and Christian missionary action are two distinct
forces, even though they are interrelated, and the former
achieved its greatest success only when it had disassociated
itself completely from the latter, as the Dutch and the English East India companies both did in their palmy days. It
is well known that the Dutch retained their trade with Japan
only by disassociating themselves entirely from Christianity,
but it is even more significant that in Ceylon they took de-
liberate measures for the restoration of Buddhist monasteries
by importing reformers from Arakan in 1684 in order to
weaken the existing native Catholicism.[6]

In the same way, in India, the East India Company, far
from acting as an agent of Christian propaganda, originally
prohibited any missionary from entering the country and
contributed to the maintenance of Hindu temples and the
celebration of religious festivals like the great Jaganath pilgrimage at Puri. It was only after the Mutiny and the trans-
ference of the dominions of the Company to the Crown that
the government of India could be said to be Christian. In
fact nowhere in India except in Goa and the Portuguese
possessions was there any attempt to use colonial power to
favour the diffusion of Christianity.

On the other hand, from 1833 onwards the English power

6 G. E. Harvey, *History of Burma*, p. 145.

in India did concern itself to promote Western education, and here the effects were far-reaching and continuous. For, as I have remarked again and again in the course of this study, the passing of European political power has done nothing to check the progress of Western education and consequently the influence of Western culture. The same thing is happening all over the East, among the peoples who have always retained their independence no less than among the ex-colonial states. If a common pan-Asian society is emerging, it is not due to any religious or philosophical synthesis, but to the new secular Westernized culture that is common to them all.

The idealization of Eastern spirituality against Western materialism, which was characteristic of the earlier phase of the nationalist movement, and which is still represented by elder statesmen like Sardar Panikkar, is being replaced by a spirit of historical criticism which shows no respect for the sacred traditions of the past.

This is especially the case in China, where the revolt against Confucius and the classical tradition took place long before the advent of Communism and is indeed the one common trait that unites the intellectual leaders of the Nationalists, like Hu Shih, and those of the Communists. Lu Hsun (1881–1936), the famous writer who is now treated as a classic by the Communists, was undoubtedly a most ferocious debunker of traditionalism and nationalism and every form of orthodoxy, but I doubt if he would have been any more sympathetic to the new Communist orthodoxy than to the old Confucian one. He is nearer in spirit to Swift than to Marx. He saw the history of China as four thousand years of cannibalism. The Confucian tradition said "Benevolence and Righteousness," but reading between the lines he found nothing but a record of man-eating. Today the totalitarian state has changed the words, but has it changed anything else? The same cannibalistic process is being carried on under the new set of slogans.

When social criticism has reached this point, there is no turning back. The old civilizations have been so violently torn from their traditional roots that it is impossible to re-vivify them. Whatever order takes their place will be something radically new, whether it is a democratic nationalism on the Western pattern or a totalitarian state. But in either case there remains a spiritual vacuum, like that we have already experienced in the secularized civilization of the Western world. I think this is already clearly discernible in the case of Lu Hsun. His discontent is plainly spiritual, rather than political or economic; even though he is not consciously aware of a religious problem. In this Lu Hsun differs considerably from writers like Wu Chih-hui in 1923, who is a real materialist, who sees the world "as a great stage on which the two-limbed animals are actors here and now. Their chief concerns in life are eating and producing children and entertaining friends. There is neither good nor evil, and neither gods nor devils. The metaphysical spectre and the religious deity are alien invaders of humanity."[7]

No doubt this is an extreme case. There are vast tracts of Asian and African society that are as yet unaffected by these revolutionary changes, as in the case of the Indian

[7] Chang Wing-tsit, *Religious Trends in Modern China* (London, Oxford; New York, Columbia University Press, 1953), p. 234.

village I have just referred to. Morever, the situation in the Islamic countries is different, owing to the close connection of religion and politics, the existence of a genuine pan-Islamic loyalty that often outweighs nationalist sentiments, and a general backwardness in industrial and technological change.

But wherever the new forces develop freely, and in proportion as the people of Asia and Africa take their equal share in the cosmopolitan civilization of the modern world, there will be a new religious need which will not be satisfied by the traditional answers of the old religious cultures.

As in the ancient world, there will be a free market in ideas and any apostle of any creed who is able to satisfy the spiritual needs of modern man will obtain a hearing. Not that the debate will be a philosophical and metaphysical one, as it was in the ancient world. This is not a metaphysical age, and in the East no less than in the West men are more interested in subsistence and coexistence than in essence and existence. Yet they still seek spiritual nourishment. There is a general sense of frustration and bewilderment and a need for a common purpose and a common hope. Up to a point the new political and national movements supply this, but not permanently and not for everyone. The deeper spiritual needs of mankind must always remain, unless we can accept George Orwell's nightmare alternative of a completely dehumanized civilization.

It is easy to understand how this state of secularization has arisen as a temporary and exceptional condition, but I do not believe that it can persist indefinitely without destroying the civilization that produced it. Religion is essential to humanity and cannot be permanently banished from the modern world.

Thus the Christian Church today and in the immediate future is confronted with a tremendous opportunity. The civilization of the new world has an immense unsatisfied spiritual need. The Church has a universal spiritual mission, which she has hitherto been unable to fulfill because the nations have been separated from one another, speaking different spiritual languages, enclosed in separate worlds, each of which has been shut off from the rest by walls of custom and tradition. Now the old barriers that divided the nations have been broken down, and the sacred laws that ruled men's lives for thousands of years have lost their power.

If Christianity were just one among the other world religions, then it too would fail and fade as they are doing. But we know that it is not so, that Christ is the only answer to the world's spiritual need, and that the Church has a universal mission to bring the Gospel of Christ to all nations.

But do we Christians today possess the power and the vision to carry out this apostolate in this new world that I have described? Although the opportunity is great, the difficulties are great also, and it will need great spiritual energy to overcome them. On the one hand, there is the negative opposition of modern secularism and materialism, which has a formidable champion in Communism and which renders all Christian action in China and Central Asia most difficult. And on the other hand there is the challenge of religious nationalism, which rejects Christianity as an alien power—an instrument of foreign domination—and identifies national loyalty with loyalty to the religious traditions of the nation. This is a paradoxical attitude in that it is political rather than religious and does not necessarily involve a revival of religious faith. It does, however, lead to an anti-missionary propaganda and an anti-Christian ideology which put serious obstacles in the way of missionary activity, above all in the sphere of education.

Neither of these two difficulties is insurmountable, but I do not think it has as yet been discovered how they can best be dealt with. Here there is need for much study, and possibly for new experiments and new techniques. I believe, however, that they can best be dealt with on a national rather than a cultural basis. For as I have explained, it is no longer a question of penetrating the closed worlds of the ancient civilizations—this work of penetration has already been done by the secular forces that have created the new oriental nationalism. It is now a matter of making a direct approach to each nation individually.

This approach may be made on a number of different planes. In the first place the most obvious approach seems to be to the new educated classes who are the creators and leaders of the modern Orient. They are the most accessible to us since they belong to the same world-society and are faced with the same problems as we are. Here Christianity enjoys a certain advantage, since it has a far greater experience of the religious problems of a secularized society than any other religion except perhaps Judaism. Moreover, the educated Asian tends to be educated in Western literature rather than in the classical literatures of the oriental cultures, and this provides a basis for mutual discussion and understanding.[8] Yet on the other hand, it is on this level that the

---

[8] I have been told that all Indonesian intellectuals read Graham Greene, though I think this must be rather an exaggeration!

nationalist and political prejudice against Christianity and
against any form of missionary activity is strongest. For the
less a man practises his own religion the more he is inclined
to resent the universal claims of Christianity.

On the other hand, the plane that is most remote from
Western influence, that of the oriental underworld—the
world of the villages and of traditional culture—is often
more accessible to missionary influence, for it is here among
the poor, the unprivileged and the outcasts, that the supernatural appeal of the Gospel is most evident. The ultimate
test of the Christian apostolate is that which was laid down
by Our Lord Himself in His message to St. John the Baptist: "The blind see, the lame walk, the lepers are made
clean, the deaf hear, the dead rise again, and the poor have
the gospel preached to them." And this principle has always
been justified by the great representatives of the Christian
apostolate from SS. Peter and Paul to St. Francis Xavier
and more recently by men like Father Damien and hundreds
of forgotten missionaries.

But in addition to these two widely separated worlds of
the intelligentsia and the peasants, there is a third intermediate sphere which is perhaps the most important of all.

For when we read the Acts of the Apostles we find that
the decisive success of the first Christian apostolate was neither with the intelligentsia nor with the peasants. St. Paul
preached alike to the sophisticated Hellenist public at Athens and to the simple peasant population of Lycaonia, who
hailed Paul and Barnabas as gods and brought out oxen and
garlands to sacrifice to them. But the world mission of the
Church was established for all time in the great urban

centres of the ancient world—at Antioch and Ephesus and Corinth and Rome and among the international lower-middle-class population of the great cities—shopkeepers, artisans, merchants, slaves and freedmen of the great houses. It was in this uprooted, denationalized, cosmopolitan population that the spiritual need was greatest and that the word was most eagerly heard and accepted. And so these cities became the centres of the new Christian world, and it was from their population that the teachers and the martyrs of the new faith came forth.

Is it not possible that the same thing will happen in modern Asia: that the key points of oriental Christianity will be found in the great urban centres like Calcutta and Bombay, Tokyo, Shanghai, Canton, Singapore—that the new Churches will find their future leaders in the same urban cosmopolitan classes from which the leaders of the primitive Church were drawn? The soil must be broken—the plough and the harrow must do their work before the seed can produce a good harvest. But this is the age of the plough and the harrow, not the time of harvest.

12

Epilogue:
The Papacy and the Modern World

The Popes of the twentieth century have been called to rule the Church in an age of revolutionary change when one catastrophe has followed upon another, when the old land marks have been submerged by the flood of change and the old rules of tradition and precedent no longer avail. During these pontificates the world has changed and the conditions of the Christian apostolate have been changed with it. A new world has come into existence, though it often seems not a world but a formless chaos, and the Church has had to find a new language in which to speak the creative word to the new nations that are being born or renewed.

In the last years of the reign of Pius IX, Rome was perhaps more isolated from the civilization of the modern world than at any previous period. The great achievements of the pontificate of Pius IX had seemed to be annulled by the political defeat of the Papacy and the destruction of the temporal power. Pius IX had become the prisoner of the Vatican and his last years were darkened by the growing alienation of the Catholic world from the Holy See. It was the age of the

Kulturkampf, the denunciation of the Austrian Concordat and the growth of militant anticlericalism in France and Italy and Latin America. In Italy Catholics could no longer take part in public life, while elsewhere they had become identified with lost causes like Carlism in Spain and royalism in France: in the eyes of a hostile world the Papacy seemed to stand alone, undefended and without allies, against the triumphant forces of modern secular civilization.

Nevertheless there were some who read the lesson of history in a very different sense. Cardinal Manning, who had been one of the foremost defenders of the temporal power in the years before 1870, was also one of the first to foresee the true nature of the change that was taking place. During his visits to Rome in these years he expressed again and again his sense that a turning point in the history of the Church had been reached, that the old world of the courts and dynasties was dead and that a new world of the peoples was coming into existence—a new Christendom which was no longer confined to Europe but was expanding across the oceans and the continents to embrace the whole habitable world.

In 1878 this new world was indeed only visible to the eye of the prophet. The world was dominated by a small group of European states and statesmen and the expansion of Western civilization represented the triumph of material power and the exploitation of a subject world by Western capitalism.

It was however in this age that Leo XIII laid the foundations of a new papal apostolate and began the great work of Christian reconstruction which has now reached its fulfilment in the work of the Papacy in the 20th century.

In the past, encyclicals and other papal utterances had possessed a somewhat limited appeal. They were read by bishops and theologians, but they did not reach the common man, nor did they deal with the problems which immediately affected the lives of the masses. But from the time of Leo XIII onwards, papal utterances have acquired a new character. Peter has spoken directly to the whole body of the faithful on the great issues which concern humanity: on modern civilization and the dangers that threaten it, on the state and its functions, on liberty and citizenship, on capitalism and socialism, on the condition of the workers and on the family as the basis of human society.

But the new apostolate to the nations which was begun by Leo XIII assumed a new character during the period after World War I. In the beginning Leo XIII was speaking to a world that was intoxicated by material power and prosperity and there were few to listen to the prophetic voice which warned Europe of the dangers that threatened society and of the abyss of destruction towards which modern society was tending. But after 1914 the whole aspect of history changed. The old securities disappeared and the dangers which Leo XIII had foreseen suddenly became monstrous realities with which European statesmen were forced to grapple and which affected the life and death of millions of common men. The catastrophe brought the Papacy and the modern world together in a new way. Not that the conflict between Christian principles and secular civilization was in any way lessened; on the contrary the revolutionary consequences of the first World War, above all in Russia, revealed more clearly than ever how deep this conflict was: but at least men could no longer feel, as they had done in the 19th century, that the Church had become detached from the contemporary world and that the teachings of the Papacy were no longer relevant to the needs of modern man. For now it became evident that the cause of the Church was the cause of humanity.

For more than a hundred years Western man has set his faith in a religion of material progress and scientific enlightenment which would free mankind from the miseries and ignorance of past ages and create an earthly paradise of freedom and prosperity. Now this dream has suddenly disappeared, and its failure was not due to any lack of power, since it occurred at a moment when Science had given Western man new powers which far surpassed his highest expectations. It was a moral and spiritual failure due to a flaw in his own nature;—a curse of Babel which divided man from man and nation from nation so that they no longer understood one another's speech but were driven to destroy one another by an instinct that was far stronger than the rational idealism in which they had put their faith. This is the curse of nationalism which, beginning in the romantic cult of the element of diversity in European culture, has spread like an epidemic from one end of the world to the other, leaving no room for an international order and no common ground on which to build a world civilization.

In this confusion of tongues, the Papacy stands as the one supranational power which can speak to the nations the words of peace and reconciliation. At first sight the Church has little reason to look with hope on this new situation. She has lost not only her old allies, the Catholic monarchies which disappeared after the first World War, but also the Christian states of Eastern Europe like Poland and Hungary which have disappeared behind the iron curtain of a totalitarian and anti-Christian imperialism. She has seen the field of her missionary activity increasingly restricted by the revolt of Asia and Africa against the West, and while Christianity has suffered from its traditional association with European culture, that culture itself has continued to become increasingly secularized and more alienated from the Christian Faith.

But these losses have been in some degree compensated by the new opportunities that have been opened to the Christian apostolate. The breakdown of the traditional association between the Church and the Catholic States with their concordats and entrenched privileges and prerogatives, has set the Papacy free to undertake its universal mission to humanity at large. The new pattern of international organization and world order has far more in common with the Catholic ideal of natural law and universal order than the old state system which rested so largely on *raison d'etat* and the claims of historical precedent. No doubt the new internationalism is secular in spirit and derives from liberal rather than Christian tradition: no doubt its action is still hampered and restricted by power politics and the power of the veto. Nevertheless the fact remains that the central principles on which the Popes had based their social teaching— the unity of the family of nations and the sovereignty of the reign of law and the principles of international justice—have now been accepted and given juridical expression by the ruling powers of the modern world. At the same time the establishment of the General Assembly of the United Nations, and the numerous subsidiary institutions for cultural and economic purposes, has created a new world forum and a new area of common activity which is at once wider and more free than the old diplomatic channels of international action.

The principles formulated by papal teaching apply not only to the relation between society and the individual, but also to the relation of societies to one another. In principle, according to the creative divine purpose for humanity, all the different societies and states and peoples form a universal community with a common purpose and common duties. Thus there is no room for state sovereignty in the absolute sense, for every state is the member of a wider society and is morally bound to cooperate with its fellows for the common good and to submit to the common law of international justice—to the law of nature and of nations.

This international society was not created by the Treaty of Versailles or the Atlantic Charter. It has always existed and looks to nature and the Creator of nature for its foundation. But there is an immense gulf between this divinely instituted and immutable order and the historical realities of international politics, in which states and nations have devoured one another, like the fishes in the sea. Throughout history war and violence have been so common that they seem the normal condition of the human race and there have been times like the early middle ages when this state of perpetual war was not confined to states and empires but was diffused throughout society, so that every city and family was in arms against its neighbour. Under these conditions the reign of law was confined to islands of order that had been created and defended by the sword. For the sword is the traditional symbol of sovereignty and it was only under its shadow that human justice was administered. At the same time even in the darkest ages mankind retained a consciousness of the divine origins of justice and of the duty of the bearer of the sword to use his power in the service of God. And as the Church extended her influence over the barbarian kingdoms of Europe, there grew up a Christian Society of Nations which recognized, at least in principle, that they were bound by a common law of justice, so that the evil realities of war and despotism were no longer the only reality, but were regarded as the social expression of the moral disorder in which human nature has been involved from the beginning.

In the modern world both these two opposing tendencies are still represented, though today they have assumed new forms. On the one hand, as Pius XII pointed out in his first great encyclical—*Summi Pontificatus*—the secularization of modern civilization has brought darkness on the earth and has set up in a new form the old bloodstained idols which Christianity had cast out. The totalitarian state involves not only the denial of personal liberty and the freedom of conscience, it is also irreconcilable with international peace and order, since it puts itself outside the family of nations and denies the existence of any higher law than the law of revolutionary violence. And the same errors are found in the exaggerated forms of nationalism, which substitute nationality for humanity as the ultimate source of social values, and exalt the way of life of a particular people above the universal moral law.

But this is only one side of the picture, for the same age which has seen the secularization of Western culture and the rise of the totalitarian state, has also witnessed the development of a world-wide movement making for international order and cooperation. The influence of this movement is not confined to the two great official experiments in world government—the League of Nations and the United Nations Organization. It also manifests itself at many different levels in international movements for humanitarian, economic, scientific, and cultural ends; and though these are now being brought into relation with the United Nations Organization, many of them are independent in origin and date back to the last century.

All this is a new phenomenon. It may have been inspired to some extent by the example and influence of Christianity, but it is not the conscious product of Christian principles, like the common institutions of medieval Christendom.

Nevertheless it is an unfortunate fact that internationalism, like the humanitarianism with which it is so closely allied, is a relatively superficial movement, which represents the aspirations of the idealist or the moralist; whereas totalitarianism and ultra-nationalism are inspired by the deeper irrational forces in human nature which manifest themselves in war and revolution.

Thus the soul of modern civilization is divided between the sublimated abstractions of humanity and international unity and scientific enlightenment which are apparent to the reason, and the repressed forces of revolution and violence which move the passions and the will to power; and

humanity will perish in the conflict unless some higher
spiritual power intervenes.

As the Church in the Dark Ages provided the spiritual
motive power which transformed the warring chaos of the
barbarian world into the European commonwealth of nations, so to-day the Church remains the only power which is
capable of overcoming the spiritual disorder of the modern
world and making the Society of Nations a living organic
reality. No doubt this international mission will be regarded
by secular opinion as remote from the political realities of the
modern world. If the Catholic Church can no longer maintain its old unquestioned authority in Christian Europe, if
Christendom no longer exists as a social reality, how can we
expect to see the extension of her influence over the nations
that have never known her, or have been divided from her by
centuries of conscious opposition? In the past moreover, the
Church was able to extend her influence into the non-
Christian world through the alliance and protection of the
colonial and imperial powers: as we see in the case of the
Spanish empire in America, the Portuguese patriarchate in
Asia, and the Austrian empire and the Polish kingdom in
Eastern Europe. But to-day these powers no longer exist and
the very memory of their achievements is an embarrassment
when the old cultures of Asia and the new nationalism of
Africa are in revolt against the West and the traditions of
European colonisation. Yet in spite of all these difficulties
there has been no weakening in the Church's insistence on
the universality of her mission. On the contrary she has
redoubled her missionary activities during the present century, and the decline of power and influence of Western

Christendom has brought out more clearly than ever her international or rather supranational character as the one universal society in which the spiritual unity of the human race is realized.

For secular internationalism, in spite of the hope of peace that it offers, is at once a lower and more abstract thing than the universal spiritual society whose feet are firmly planted in history and whose Head is divine: a Society which possesses no less objective reality and juridical form than a State, while at the same time its action extends to the very depths of the individual human soul.

In his Christmas allocution to the College of Cardinals in 1945 Pius XII spoke as follows:

"The Catholic Church, of which Rome is the centre, is supra-national by its very nature. . . . The Church is a mother—*Sancta Mater Ecclesia*—a true mother, mother of all nations and all peoples, no less than of all men individually. And precisely because she is a mother, she does not and cannot belong exclusively to this or that people, nor even more to some than others, but equally to all."

And the Holy Father then went on to describe how the growing individualism and totalitarianism of the modern state has made it more vital than ever to assert this supra-national character which is no longer centered in Europe and the old society of Western Christendom, but which has extended its sphere of action to include the other continents. And he concludes:

"Is there not revealed in this progressive enrichment of the supernatural and even the natural life of mankind the true significance of the Church's supra-national character? She is

not because of this supra-national character, placed aloft, as
though suspended in an inaccessible and intangible isolation
above the nations; for just as Christ was in the midst of men,
so too His Church in which He continues to live, is placed in
the midst of the peoples. As Christ assumed a real human
nature, so too the Church takes to herself the fullness of all
that is genuinely human, wherever and however she finds it,
and transforms it into a source of supernatural energy.

"Thus ever more fully is verified in the Church of today
that phenomenon which St. Augustine praised in his City of
God: 'The Church recruits her citizens from all nations and
in every language assembles her community of pilgrims upon
earth. She is not anxious about diversities in customs, laws
and institutions, she does not exclude or destroy any of them
but rather preserves and observes them. Even the differences
in different nations, so long as they do not impede the
worship of the one supreme God, she directs to the one common end of peace upon earth.' "

This universal mission to the nations is something quite
different from the relation of Church to State which has been
the main centre of attention in the past and which has given
rise to so much discussion and controversy. The State is the
juridical organization of social and military power; while the
nation represents the natural organic community of speech
and culture into which a man is born and from which he
receives the indelible imprint of a particular social tradition.
The number of states is limited and their importance is
determined by official status and protocol. But the nations
and peoples of the earth are countless and their only title to
recognition is the mere fact of their existence. They may be

the creators of world empires or lost tribes that have been thrust aside out of the stream of history. But whatever they are, strong or weak, civilized or barbarian, they all alike possess their place in the Church's universal mission. Each has its own language and its own way of life and the Church calls on them all to hear the words of life in their own tongue and to use their way of life as a way to the service of God.

This Christian internationalism with its ideal of spiritual unity in national diversity stands in contrast and opposition to the totalitarian pattern of world order which threatens the existence not only of Christianity but of humanity itself. But this danger is not entirely due to the aggressive action of those ideological dictatorships like Communism which aim deliberately at world conquest. They have their ultimate source in certain tendencies in modern culture which are world-wide and which are growing stronger in proportion as the world is drawn together by economic and political forces. The new powers created by modern science have made the technological organization of life more complicated and more all-embracing, while on the other hand the development of democracy has made publicity and the formation and influence of mass opinion the dominant forces in social life.

These forces are not in themselves evil, so long as they are subordinated to rational and moral ends, but as soon as they get out of control or are exploited recklessly in the interests of power by parties or groups, they become engines of social destruction. Any society that submits to their unrestricted action becomes a huge machine which crushes human nature under its pressure and uses the disintegration of the mind and will of the individual human person as a source of inhuman energy.

This process of degeneration and destruction affects the life of nations as well as individuals, since, as Pius XII has observed, the totalitarian order destroys that continuity in time which has hitherto been regarded as an essential condition of life in society, so that man is cut off from his social past and left isolated to face the enormous pressure of contemporary materialism.

Now it is the consciousness of continuity in time, of the living past and the social inheritance, that makes a nation and a social culture. If the nations are deprived of this, they are no more than masses—human herds separated from one another by the barriers of language, and submitted blindly to the absolute control of forces which possess unlimited technological power and resources, but which are themselves blind, because they lack spiritual knowledge and direction. In this dark world, divided against itself, cursed by the confusion of tongues and frustrated by the lack of common purpose, the Papacy speaks to the nations as the representative of the only power that can "lead man back from the shadows into the light. The Church alone can make him conscious of the past, master of the present, and secure for the future. Like the mother of a family, she daily gathers around her all her sons scattered over the world and brings them into the unity of her vital Divine Principle." (Pius XII, Allocution of Feb. 20, 1946.)

This profound doctrine of the supra-national mission of the Church as the centre of spiritual unity in a divided humanity has been developed and actualized by the Popes of the twentieth century throughout the course of their apostolic ministry. In countless utterances and public audiences they have applied these principles to the special needs and circumstances of the different peoples. Never perhaps in the history of the Church have the peoples come to Rome in such numbers and from so many different regions, and in addition a still wider world audience has been reached by the radio and television and all the resources of modern publicity.

We seem to see the beginnings of a new Pentecostal dispensation by which again "all men hear in their own tongues the wonderful works of God." The pontificates of the twentieth century have been a catastrophic period, full of wars and the rumours of wars and the distress of nations, but they have also seen the dawn of a new hope for humanity. They foreshadow the birth of a new Christendom—a Society which is not confined as in the past to a single group of nations and a single civilization but which is common to every people and language and unites all the members of the human family in the divine community of the Mystical Body of Christ.

Appendix

Chapters in other books by Christopher Dawson on (1) Oriental religion and culture, and (2) relationships between East and West

Abbreviations

Age: The Age of the Gods (1926) (Reprinted by Howard Fertig, Inc., 80 East 11th St., New York, NY 10003)

P&R: Progress & Religion (1929) (Reprinted by Greenwood Press, Inc., 51 Riverside Ave., Westport CT 06880)

Mak: The Making of Europe (1932)

R&C: Religion & Culture (1947: Vol. I of Dawson's Gifford Lectures. Reprinted by AMS Press, Inc., 56 East 13th St., New York, NY 10003)

UE: Understanding Europe (1952)

Med.: Medieval Essays (1954) (Reprinted by Arno Press, 3 Park Ave., New York NY 10016.)

Dyn.: Dynamics of World History (1958) (Republished with a new Preface (1978) by John J. Mulloy. 510 pp. $7.95. Sherwood Sugden & Company, 1117 Eighth St., La Salle, IL 61301.)

HRCC: The Historic Reality of Christian Culture (1960) (Greenwood Press, above.)

Form.: The Formation of Christendom (1967)

Enq.: Enquiries into Religion & Culture (1933) (Arno Press, above.)

R&WH: Religion & World History (1975)

I. Oriental Sacred Society and the Rise of Civilization:

The Neolithic Culture and the Religion of the Peasant (*Age*, ch. 5)

The City State and the Development of the Sumerian Culture (*Age*, ch. 6)

The Archaic Culture in Egypt and the Development of the Great State (*Age*, ch. 7)

The Age of Empire in the Near East (*Age*, ch. 13) (Includes Ikhnaton)

Religion and the Origins of Civilization (*P&R*, ch. 5; second half deals with Near Eastern religion-cultures)

The Warrior Peoples and the Decline of the Archaic Civilization (*Dyn.*, art. 12)

The Religious Organs of Society: Kingship (*R&C*, ch. 6. Pp. 115-128 deal with Egypt and the Near East.)

II. The Rise of the Oriental World Religions

The Rise of the World Religions (*P&R*, ch. 6)

Confucius and the Tao (*R&WH*, ch. 4)

Mysticism in India (*R&WH*, ch. 5)

Zoroaster in Persia (*R&WH*, ch. 6)

The Development of Greek Thought (*R&WH*, ch. 7. Includes oriental influences.)

The Religious Organs of Society: Priesthood and Sacrifice (*R&C*, ch. 5. Pp. 92-101 deal with these concepts in Indian religion.)

The Divine Order and the Social Order (*R&C*, ch. 8. Pp. 161-172 treat this concept as found in Confucianism and Taoism.)

The Divine Order and the Spiritual Life (*R&C*, ch. 9. Pp. 179-193 show this concept in the Upanishads, Buddhism, and the Gita.)

III. Judaism and Christianity Against their Oriental Background

The Christian and Jewish Idea of Revelation (*Form.*, ch. 5. Unique character of O.T. Jewish development and its inheritance by Christianity.)

The Coming of the Kingdom (*Form.*, ch. 6)

Christianity and the Greek World (*Form.*, ch. 7. Conflict of Christianity with Oriental religious ideas in Hellenistic world.)

The Catholic Church (*Mak.*, ch. 2. Early Church maintains its identity against Oriental influences.)

The Roman Empire and the Birth of the Christian Church (*R&WH*, Pt. II, ch. 2)

IV. Byzantium and the Christian East

The Christian East and the Oriental Background of Christian Culture (*Med.*, ch. 2)

The Christian Empire and the Rise of the Byzantine Culture (*Mak.*, ch. 6)

The Awakening of the East and the Revolt of the Subject Nationalities (*Mak.*, ch. 7)

The Byzantine Renaissance and the Revival of the Eastern Empire (*Mak.*, ch. 10)

The Christian Empire (*Form.*, ch. 8)

Liturgy and Theology in Byzantine Culture (*Form.*, ch. 9)

East and West in the Middle Ages (*Form.*, ch. 17)

The Byzantine Tradition and the Conversion of Eastern Europe (*Religion and the Rise of Western Culture*, ch. 6)

V. Islam

The Rise of Islam (*Mak.*, ch. 8)

The Expansion of Moslem Culture (*Mak.*, ch. 9)

Islamic Mysticism (*Enq.*, art. 10)

The Moslem West and the Oriental Background of Later Medieval Culture (*Med.*, ch. 7)

The Origins of the Romantic Tradition (*Med.*, ch. 11. Influence of Arab

thought and poetry on Western medieval Romance literature.)
The Growth and Diffusion of Culture (*Form.*, ch. 4. Pp. 55-63 deal with
Islam as a superculture.)
The Religious Organs of Society: Prophets and Divination (*R&C*, ch. 4.
Pp. 72-81; 84 deal with Islam as outstanding example of the proph-
etic element in religion.)

VI. Asia and the West

Cycles of Civilization (*Enq.*, art. 5)
Religion and the Life of Civilization (*Enq.*, art. 6)
The Friars' Mission to the Mongols (Introd. to *The Mongol Mission*)
Russia and Asia (*UE*, ch. 6)
Asia and Europe (*UE*, ch. 7)
Europe Overseas: Colonization and Empire (*UE*, ch. 8)
The Mystery of China (*Enq.*, art. 8)
Civilization in Crisis (*HRCC*, ch. 6. Pp. 79-85 deal with this crisis as
found in Oriental societies.)
Is the Church Too Western? (*HRCC*, ch. 8)
Europe in Eclipse (*Dyn.*, last article)
See also in the present volume, "The Relevance of European History,"
and the six chapters included in the section, "Asia and the West."

VII. Christianity Compared with the Oriental World Religions

The Nature and Destiny of Man (*Enq.*, last article, secs. II to V)
Stages in Mankind's Religious Experience (*Dyn.*, art. 15)
Christianity and the Rise of Western Civilization (*P&R*, ch. 7, first half
shows contrast of Christian and Jewish worldview with that of
Orient.)
See also the "Foreword" to the present volume, and the "View of World
History," pp. 457-468 of the *Dynamics of World History*, both written by
J.J.M., with quotations on this topic from Dawson's books and letters.

From the same publisher:

Dynamics of World History by Christopher Dawson. 509 pages. Paper. $7.95.
Christianity in East and West by Christopher Dawson. Paper: $4.95.
Escape from Scepticism: Liberal Education as if Truth Mattered by Christopher Derrick. Paper:
$2.95.
Joy Without a Cause: Selected Essays of Christopher Derrick. Paper: $4.95.
Beyond Détente: Toward an American Foreign Policy by Paul Eidelberg. Cloth: $12.95.
A Better Guide Than Reason: Studies in the American Revolution by M. E. Bradford. Cloth: $12.95;
paper: $4.95.
Citizen of Rome: Reflections from the Life of a Roman Catholic by Frederick D. Wilhelmsen. 345
pages. Paper: $5.95.
The Prophetic Poet and the Spirit of the Age: Volume I: *Why Flannery O'Connor Stayed Home* by
Marion Montgomery. 488 pages. Cloth: $19.95. Volume II: *Why Poe Drank Liquor.*
Cloth: $19.95. Volume III: *Why Hawthorne Was Melancholy.* Cloth: $19.95.
The Impatience of Job by George W. Rutler. Paper: $3.95.
(All prices include postage & handling.)